The
Forgotten Cost
Of
Freedom

by

Eric J. Kiser

<u>DEDICATION</u>

This book is dedicated to my Family.
To my Mother, Audrey, who gave me my sense of humor.
To my Father, Thomas, who gave me my sense of honor.
To my Sisters, Karen & Marilyn, who gave me almost everything else
And to Annie, I miss you every day.
I love you all!

CONTENTS

ACKNOWLEDGMENTS

I gratefully acknowledge everyone who helped me write this book in a million different ways: My Mom and Dad who gave feedback on early drafts and who always encouraged me to write. Karen and Marilyn who listened to me ramble as I worked through my thoughts and defined my positions. Stu Segall; who wasn't the first person to tell me to "quit complaining and write a book" but was probably the most persuasive. Scott H. Silverman whose work, as I see it, is the gold standard for anyone who questions whether one person can make a difference, and whose friendship inspired me to push forward on this project. Paul Raymer, PhD, Francis Raymer and their son Tim, who will probably never know how much I enjoy sitting and talking with them on just about any subject, but most especially politics. My fellow members of 'The League of Non-Aligned Voters', for constantly encouraging me, and the confidence they have in my ability to be their voice. Finally, Mike Dobbyn, for teaching me as much about life as he ever did about high school math, then after all these years, agreeing to help edit these pages. But mostly for being someone I am proud to call friend. I could not have done this without every single one of you. Thank you all.

INTRODUCTION

"Government is instituted for the common good; for the protection, safety, prosperity, and happiness of the people; and not for profit, honor, or private interest of any one man, family, or class of men; therefore, the people alone have an incontestable, unalienable, and indefeasible right to institute government; and to reform, alter, or totally change the same, when their protection, safety, prosperity, and happiness require it."

~ *John Adams, Thoughts on Government, 1776*

꘎ ꘎ ꘎

When I decided to write this book the approval rating for the President of the United States was a low 36% and the congressional approval rating was at a dismal 14%. The mood of the nation was, and continues to be, general disgust for our representatives and a strong desire for change.

Unfortunately, the answer these days seems to be to choose a politician from one of the legislative bodies and somehow trust they will bring about the needed improvements or reforms. The American people have no idea how to create the necessary change, so they end up putting their hope and trust into a single individual or one political party to do it for them. Meanwhile, these political parties have managed to convince the majority of Americans that the fault for all our problems lays squarely in the lap of their opposition. Do we really believe that one party has all the answers? Or that the other is the cause of every problem on earth? I don't think so. Could it be that each side has some ideas or platforms that are good for America, and some that are bad? This seems a little more accurate to me. But the most likely scenario is that each political party shares much of the blame for the problems of our current political system and both have a vested interest in maintaining the status quo.

I believe that as Americans we have truly lost our way. It is not that we don't want to make things better. We do. Instead, I believe that we simply do not know how to go about righting this ship of state. We were never taught how to go about this in school. Besides, we have our own lives to live, so how can we take the time to go about creating change when we don't know how to make it happen in the first place? Well, I can tell you right off the bat that the answer does not lie with a single person, political party or any group who says they are going to change the world all by themselves. This simply is not realistic. It sure would be nice if it were true, because then the rest of us would not have to worry about it and we could go back to our couch's to finish watching "Dancing with the Stars". Ultimately, we do have to worry about it, and in the end, we will be the ones to blame if this experiment called representative government fails.

I believe that in order to correct the problems in our federal government today we must first understand how the United States became viewed as one of the greatest nations to exist on Earth. Did this happen by chance? Did it happen because we have a greater lock on the truth than other countries? Did we just get lucky? And has our luck run out? The truth is that there were very clear concepts and principles that caused our nation to rise to the top and reasons that are just as clear as too why we are slipping from that peak. It is my opinion that we have forgotten what those principles are or perhaps this generation never fully understood them in the first place.

Instead of seeking to understand the core philosophical foundation of this nation -- what made it so great in the first place -- most people seem to be making emotional decisions based upon factors that have a) little impact b) no impact, or c) exactly the wrong kind of impact on the problem being addressed. To make matters worse, Americans today are choosing their leaders based upon some television version of charisma or if their candidate seems "presidential." (really! "seems" presidential!). Americans can't be bothered with facts, figures, plans or policies so they make decisions based upon how a particular candidate makes them feel while watching 3 minutes of coverage on the nightly news. This should scare the hell out of us. Having spent most of my career in the industry, I can tell you one thing for sure; how something is presented to the public by the media bears very little resemblance to how that thing actually is.

In trying to understand our current situation, and in searching for solutions, I created what I think of as a "handbook" that can be used to assess most of the major problems we face in government today and how we can go about using the constitution and common sense to address them going forward. The problem is that each one of these issues will require hard work and a greater understanding on the part of the American people and I am just not convinced we are willing to put forth the time and effort required. That is why I titled this book: "The Forgotten Cost of Freedom" because I think the citizens of this country have forgotten that there is a price that must be paid to maintain true freedom and to ensure that our government continues to run as it was originally intended. I hope I am wrong. However, if I am not and it turns out that we really are unwilling to pay that price, then we must accept what we get and we really should stop complaining.

I have written this book with one goal in mind, to attempt to get more Americans thinking about regaining control over their government again. In the process, I suggest ways on how to do that by removing emotion from the equation and replacing it with logic and common sense. If we can put away our partisanship long enough to consider these, and hopefully a few other, concepts then perhaps we can all come to a greater understanding of the work that we have to do. At the very least, I hope I can get you to reassess your current commitment to fixing the problem and encourage you to demand the rights and freedoms that you were guaranteed by those who came before you.

I have broken this book down into six main "costs" that we all must pay for the freedom we enjoy and examples of how we can go about maintaining those freedoms. I have also offered up a few potential solutions to many of the problems we face today. Some of them you may have heard before. But I think you will find most of them somewhat new and hopefully a little innovative. I also try to share with you several experiences from my life that, while I hope you find humorous, have taught me a lot about human nature and the way I believe is best to go about using the government to solve problems and address issues. I have also included in the final chapter some ideological information on a group I am affiliated with who welcome all ideas, regardless of political affiliation, from folks who are interested in preserving the core ideals of the United States of America for future generations.

It is my most sincere hope that after reading this book you will consider some of these things in a different light and then decide for yourself whether you see the value of fixing this country or not. Then I hope you will make a personal assessment of how much you currently are, or might be willing to pay, for the freedoms you enjoy.

Eric J. Kiser.

1.
THE PRICE OF DOING BUSINESS

"They that can give up essential liberty to purchase a little temporary safety deserve neither liberty nor safety."

~ *Benjamin Franklin, Historical Review of Pennsylvania, 1759*

———————————————— ✦ ————————————————

On Monday, December 8, 1980 Mark David Chapman, a 25-year-old security guard from Honolulu, Hawaii, came to New York City to murder music legend John Lennon. Chapman had suffered from mental health problems for many years and became obsessed with the religious and political messages of Lennon's music. As Lennon and his wife, Yoko Ono, exited their limousine and headed toward their home, Chapman stepped out of the shadows and fired five rounds from a Charter Arms .38 Special into Lennon's back killing him almost instantly.

Approximately 31 years later, on January 8, 2011, Congresswoman Gabrielle Giffords was the victim of an assassination attempt at a grocery store near Tucson, AZ. She was meeting publicly with her constituents as part of the "Congress on your Corner" program when a man ran up to the crowd and began firing. The gunman, identified as Jared Lee Loughner, shot 19 people, of which six died immediately. Among the dead was conservative Federal Judge John Roll. Giffords managed to survive even after being critically injured by a gunshot wound to the head. Bystanders detained the suspected shooter, whose motives remain unclear although he seems to have been fixated on the Congresswoman, until he was taken into police custody. Loughner was later judged "Incompetent to Stand Trial" but that ruling is set to be re-assessed in late 2012.

In our free society, we have been and will always be confronted with great challenges such as attempted assassinations, school shootings, crime, etc. How we choose to deal with these challenges truly defines who we are as a nation and who we will become. This is why it is critical that, as Americans, we have a clear understanding of where our freedoms come from and that they have a cost associated with them. Immediately following each of the horrible events described above there was a cry for new laws and legislative changes to ensure that these types of events could never happen again. While it is always important to analyze why tragedies happen and to try to reduce the possibility of re-occurrence, there is an inherent risk of going too far in the name of safety or some fleeting sense of security. In the process, we tend to reduce the very freedoms that are the cornerstone of our society. An important thing to understand is that in doing this our nation has consistently reduced our freedom over the years. Even more important is the realization that these changes have *NEVER* achieved the desired effect of reducing or stopping the problem that induced the legislation in the first place.

This chapter contains the single most important concept for the enduring survival of our free society -- Freedom comes at a price. It always has and it always will. If we are to protect our freedom as the incredible gift that was bestowed upon us by the founders of this country, we must understand that cost and be willing to pay the price with our lives. Failure to do so will render the greatest experiment in democracy, the United States of America, a lesson in futility. The important principle that every American must understand is that:

--The *GREATEST* cost we are expected to pay to ensure our freedom is that there will *ALWAYS* be those who choose to abuse that freedom! --

Continued ignorance of this core principle has resulted in the chipping away of the most basic freedoms that we once enjoyed. The great irony is that this purposeful degradation of freedom has all been accomplished in the name of protecting our freedoms and keeping us safe -- yet neither goal has been achieved in the process. Because most Americans seemingly do not understand the most important cost of our freedom we have allowed and even encouraged the removal of those freedoms. This is why I believe that it is time to set the record straight! It is time that we all understand what our freedoms cost so that we can choose to pay the price instead of destroying our freedom in the name of protecting ourselves from potential danger.

This incredibly important concept is really quite simple when put in the proper perspective. Here's how it works; If we want the freedom to drive a vehicle we must accept the idea that someone may make an error behind the wheel of another vehicle and strike your automobile, causing damage or even death. If we desire the right to bear arms then we must accept the possibility that someone may use a gun to rob us or kill us. If we desire the right to consume alcohol then we must concede that someone may drive while under the influence of alcohol and kill one of us or a member of our family. This basic acceptance of the potential consequences of our freedoms is the most fundamental understanding we can have in a free society.

The important question is "Are we willing to pay the price any longer?" Today our representatives seem to think that it is possible to remove the cost of our freedoms while still preserving the freedom itself. Unfortunately, this is impossible even though it sounds wonderful. Certainly, there are things that can be done to regulate these freedoms in order to mitigate the costs but in the end, if we want the freedom, we must be willing to accept the cost. There just is no other way around it.

The question for our government then becomes "How do we deal with the abuse of freedom when it occurs without removing the associated right altogether?" In other words, how do we keep people from using firearms to commit crimes while still protecting the right to own guns? Or, how do we keep people from driving while under the influence of alcohol while still protecting the right to consume liquor or beer? These questions have been asked since the very beginnings of our nation and will continue to be asked as long as man seeks freedom on this earth. The problem is that if we do not clearly understand how freedom works, and what costs are associated with them, we will eventually give them away freely because a world without gun violence or drunken driving deaths sounds appealing and even naively achievable. The sad reality is that we have become so backwards in our society that we applaud when we lose our rights in the name of protecting freedoms -- thinking that somehow this is the answer to our problem.

Politicians today are elected based upon party rhetoric and campaign promises that can only result in the loss of one freedom after another. Think about it. Lawmakers and legislatures are designed to do one thing: pass legislation and make new laws. The only reason this is allowed to happen is that our representatives, and the people of this nation, have forgotten the proper way to deal with the abuse of freedom when it occurs.

So, how are we supposed to deal with the abuse of freedom? What is the proper answer when guns are used to commit crime or when the abuse of alcohol results in the loss of life? Once again, the answer really is not that complicated. But, it is an answer that many people simply will not want to hear because it's not "sexy" and because, by necessity, in order to protect our basic rights, we must leave ourselves open to potential abuse and people don't like that idea. The only correct answer available when dealing with an abuse of freedoms should always be:

-- "Punish those who have abused their freedom, instead of taking those freedoms away from everyone." --

How is it possible to protect rights by taking those rights away? It's not. Therefore, in the case of drunk driving, we have established a criminal justice system that punishes those who drive while under the influence of alcohol. In the case of the right to bear arms we have laws that punish those who use guns to commit crimes. In other words- in order to protect freedoms for every citizen, we must wait until an abuse happens before the law kicks in. That is how the system works.

Lately we have allowed a reverse approach to enter the debate and even legislation that strips us of our rights without any argument. Once again, it is all done in the name of saving lives and protecting rights. If people are being killed by guns, then today's answer is to remove the right to bear arms such as the handgun ban in Washington, DC. If people are being killed by drunk drivers, then we need to set up sobriety checkpoints and inconvenience everyone to ensure they are following the law. These ideas fly in the face of everything that makes a free society great and truly free.

Freedoms greatest price is that bad things can and will happen, if we intend to allow the people to remain free. For hundreds of years we embraced this fact. However, that is all changing now as we hear cries far and wide demanding the removal of rights for the greater good and in the name of saving lives. Please note-

---- The purpose of government is *NOT* to save lives! The purpose of government *IS* to preserve the *RIGHTS* of its citizens! ----

Does this concept seem strange to you? Could this be? Is it because those who seek to represent us today are always making promises about how much better government can make your life as if that is the true role of government. Let me flash you back to a famous statement from history to add a little bit of perspective, "Give me liberty or give me death!" Sound familiar? Well, it should! The emphasis in this famous statement is on rights; not life. Yes, the government does have the job of protecting our borders, and yes, it does have the responsibility of keeping someone else from taking away your rights through assault, theft, murder, etc. But how does it make sense for the government to protect you from someone who wants to take away your rights by taking away the very rights it's supposed to be protecting in the first place? It doesn't!

This is why true freedom has inherent risks and the response to those risks cannot be to take away our freedom. Instead, the goal should be to create a system that catches and punishes those who abuse their freedoms. I cannot tell you how saddened I am when I hear citizens say they are willing to give up certain rights if it means they'll be just a bit little safer -- or if it will save even one life. I am saddened because the people who make these statements clearly do not understand the founding principles of this country. More importantly, they have failed to understand that the surrender of rights has almost never resulted in the desired safety. In order to punish the abuse of freedom, we have a Criminal Justice System, which is dedicated to reducing the misuse and abuse of freedom.

"The Constitution is not an instrument for the government to restrain the people, it is an instrument for the people to restrain the government."

~ Patrick Henry

The Criminal Justice System

The Criminal Justice System has several stated goals in how it limits the abuse of freedom. They are as follows:

The first goal: is to create a deterrent to the abuse of freedom by establishing significant punishments for crime and advertising those punishments to every citizen. (Many people who consider committing crimes decide against it out of fear of the potential punishment. While this practice does not always work, detailed studies have shown there to be a consistent deterrent factor in the knowledge that the commission of a crime could possibly result in a long prison sentence.)

The second goal: is to identify criminals and apprehend them. (Obviously, this will never be a perfect system as some criminals will never be stopped or apprehended. Additionally, there are resource limitations due to a limited supply of enforcement personnel and tax funds to locate criminals and fight crime.)

The third and final goal of the Criminal Justice System: is to protect the larger community against those who abuse these freedoms by removing them from society and incarcerating them. (Unfortunately, you will note that I left out reforming criminals as a stated goal. I do this for one reason; I do not believe that our current system does any such thing. I strongly believe that reformation is an important effort, although I do not believe that it is a primary concern when discussing the protection of rights. The high amount of recidivism illustrates that our criminal justice system does not effectively reform offenders. However, even though the reformation of the criminal is not the main objective of the justice system, I do believe our system can, and should, do a better job of ensuring criminal reform. Later in this section, I will outline one possible way this could be done.)

Once again, as stated in the goals above, the actual role of our government's criminal justice system is to define crime, apprehend suspects and punish those judged guilty of abusing their freedom. Not to take away freedom from everyone because of the abuse of a few.

So, how do we go about making sure the system is working as the founders intended? One way is anytime we hear our lawmakers suggesting a new law or ban; we should ask the following questions:

1) Does the proposed law create a deterrent to crime through punishing the abuse of the freedom involved? Or

2) Does the legislation take away the freedom from all or limit that freedom because of the abuses of the few?

As we look at current legislation, we find that most of the laws being proposed in answer to the abuses of freedom are designed to take away or limit the freedoms of everyone instead of punishing only those who have abused their freedom. In essence, we are punishing all citizens and treating them as though they are guilty of a crime without the opportunity to prove their innocence. (Prove their innocence?!) In the case of sobriety checkpoints, citizens are pulled over without cause and forced to prove they are not intoxicated. On top of that, both drivers and passengers are run through the police computer system for any outstanding legal issues or warrants, which have nothing to do with drinking and driving. Private citizens can be detained or arrested without breaking the specific law these checkpoints were set up to enforce. This creates various privacy issues and is a violation of the probable cause statutes yet we do nothing to stop it. This new practice flies in the face of everything this nation stands for and goes directly against the grain of a free society.

One good warning sign that a suggested law is going in the wrong direction is if you hear the proponent of the new legislation say that it will save lives. Once again, the goal of government is to save rights; not save lives If you don't agree with this concept, consider for a moment all the lives we could save by limiting the rights of the people. How many lives could be saved by banning junk food, eliminating cigarettes and alcohol, instituting mandatory diets, body fat indexes or weight limits, getting rid of cars or limiting the ability to speed, getting rid of ladders, bathtubs, etc.. Did you know that four people lose their lives every year to accidents with vending machines? Or, that chocolate has been found to cause cancer in laboratory mice? That religion has cost more human lives than almost any other cause throughout history. Does this mean we ban vending machines, eliminate chocolate or outlaw God? Of course not. But consider this: If the true goal of government is to save lives, then it is really doing a very poor job.

Rights vs. Safety or Protecting Lives

This idea of protecting rights over safety is so important to understand that I find the need to drive it home. I use a modern day example of how it is properly executed in our society -- this time to the possible detriment of United States citizens-- to try to make a point. Remember that the reasoning behind much of today's proposed legislation is that it will save lives. Please consider this idea while you look at the following scenario-

Let's say for the sake of argument that a dangerous serial killer is loose on the streets of your hometown. Let's also say that the police apprehend the killer and actually find pictures, in the killer's storage locker, of the suspect committing the offense. Seems like an open and shut case, right? But wait, suppose that the police identified the killer through illegal wiretaps or raided his storage locker without a warrant and without probable cause. Is the judge going to allow the evidence of the killer committing the crime to be admitted into evidence? If the safety and security of the people is the paramount concern of the law then, even though the police officers broke the law, the evidence would be admitted and the killer would go to jail.

However, that is not what would happen in real life. Instead the judge would be forced to throw out the evidence and to put the killer back on the streets because the Constitution was violated in obtaining the evidence. While this may seem absolutely crazy, it is done because the role of government is to protect the rights of its citizens. If we allow the evidence to stand in this case, then we are empowering the police to search any home in America without repercussions, which would leave the government unchecked in its power. Therefore, in this case, we would put citizens at risk, by releasing this known serial killer back onto the streets, in order to protect our Constitutional rights.

In order to properly understand the correct implementation of this theme let's take a look at a few important issues facing lawmakers today and how they're dealing with these problems in comparison to what the proper response should be.

Gun Control

The demand for greater gun control is a microcosm of this theme of taking away rights instead of protecting freedom. Even though the Constitution provides for the right to bear arms there are alarming numbers of citizens and lawmakers who believe that this right should be removed because the freedom is so abused. The Problem is that unless we take away other rights along with the right to bear arms, then banning firearms will be of little use.

"Laws Are Only for the Law Abiding"

My father taught this to me from an early age. But, for many this principle is difficult to understand because it does not fall in line with our emotional logic. Surely, if there is a law abolishing guns then people will follow it, right? Well, aren't there laws against murder on the books right now? Isn't it against the law to use a firearm to commit a crime as we speak? Of course it is. So why is it that these crimes still happen? Because only law-abiding citizens follow the law and a law banning guns will only keep the law abiding from getting a weapon while criminals will not be deterred. Additionally, a law banning guns sends a message loud and clear to potential criminals that law-abiding citizens cannot protect themselves. All they need to do is get a gun. And they will!

"One loves to possess arms, though they hope never to have occasion for them."
~ Thomas Jefferson, June 19, 1796

Do you believe that the Federal government can keep illegal guns off the streets? Well, has it been able to keep illegal drugs off the streets? Just look at the statistics of our governments "war on drugs" for the answer. So why would you believe that guns would be any different?

There is a very clear reason why our government cannot control guns, or drugs, or any other illegal activity. It's this thing we like to call the Bill of Rights. As I will explain in further detail later on, the Bill of Rights and the Constitution do not limit the rights of the people. Instead, they limit the powers of government. This was the intent of our founding fathers in order to keep a potentially corrupt government in check. The Bill of Rights protects individuals from an unlawful search and seizure unless there is probable cause and a warrant. This is precisely why we will never control illegal guns or illegal substances on the street. We can mitigate their importation and try to keep the problems they cause to a minimum, but unless we do away with the protection from illegal search and seizure, we will never be able to control the importation of these items because criminals hide behind these rights in order to conceal their activities.

If we cannot control illegal guns, what good is a law banning guns? What good does it do to tell the law-abiding citizen that they cannot purchase a firearm? In my way of thinking, this type of legislation would only serve to empower the criminal who could not care less about any laws that might get in their way. Therefore, do we take away the right from everyone because it is being abused by a few? No, we need to punish those who abused their right to bear arms.

I wonder how different the massacre at Virginia Tech College would have been, or the Chardon High School attacks in Ohio, if we were not in the practice of taking away a citizens ability to protect themselves. If you were trapped in a classroom as a gunman walked down the halls firing at anything that moves, don't you think you would wish for a Security Guard with a firearm? Even if only as a last resort? How often do you think these types of situations would happen if it was still socially acceptable for every day law-abiding citizens to carry firearms? Additionally, I have heard people say things like "we need to create 'safe zones'". Let me tell you that the very logic of a "safe zone" is completely flawed. It is based upon the idea that everyone will follow the laws or rules of said zones. Once again, only the law abiding follow the laws and a safe zone only guarantees the safety of the killer with a gun.

"Besides the advantage of being armed, which the Americans possess over the people of almost every other nation, the existence of subordinate governments, to which the people are attached and by which the militia officers are appointed, forms a barrier against the enterprises of ambition, more insurmountable than any which a simple government of any form can admit of."

~ James Madison, Federalist No. 48, February 1, 1788

In an age of terrorist attacks, mentally ill people who prey on the innocent, and just straight up "bad guys", we have announced to one and all what areas are free from protection and open to any attack one can muster. Moreover, the crazy thing about it is that we have created these "safe zones" as an exact response to those that have abused their rights in the past. This makes no sense at all! In response to an attack by someone who could not care less about the laws on the books, we are going to pass a new law saying you can't commit the attack. What a bunch of nonsense!

The sixty four thousand dollar question then becomes; "Do guns cause crime?" If you listen to those that wish to ban them, we must conclude it is the gun that causes the evil, and not the person. According to this logic if you were to take a good law abiding citizen and place a gun in his hand, all of a sudden, you will have a gun toting bank robber, right? I don't agree. I'm pretty sure if someone is determined to rob a bank but cannot get a gun, they would just use something else. Like a knife or a bomb.

Now, I strongly believe that we should consider limitations on the types of guns average people should be allowed to possess without special permits. Does the normal everyday citizen really need a fully automatic AK-47 with a 500 round clip? Or armor penetrating bullets? Probably not. I mean, just how fast is that 12 point buck and where did he get that Kevlar vest? However, there are thousands of legitimate reasons for people to own various types of guns in America today. Personal protection, sport hunting, collectors and competition shooting are just a few. Common sense and public debate is needed to determine the answer to questions like this one.

One other thing that really frustrates me in the gun debate is when anti-gun activists ask why anyone would want or need a gun -- as if it is somehow our job to prove the need. Let me explain an indispensable principle; -- Rights need neither defense nor explanation -- They are our Rights. This goes for every right we enjoy, and it is not limited to just those things mentioned in the Bill of Rights. In fact, many of the founders were against the Bill of Rights because they felt that someday people might mistakenly believe that the rights listed there are our only rights. The truth is that we have a right, or should have a right to do anything we want without explanation or justification, as long as it does not take away or impair the rights of another citizen. We should never allow ourselves to fall into the trap of having to justify the need for any particular right. Actually, it should be just the opposite. Those who wish to remove the right need to prove to us why the right should be taken away. If it cannot be readily proven that the right is directly taking away the rights of another, or has the high potential to do so, they should be laughed out the door and denied.

Why do we need guns? Because we want guns! There is no need to say any more or less than this. There is no evidence that ownership of a firearm will result in the commission of a crime. Truthfully, every law-abiding citizen has access to gun ownership as we speak. All they have to do is go down and buy one -- yet somehow most refrain. Even though guns are readily available, most citizens are not using them to commit crimes. How is this possible? Because laws only affect the law abiding! This principle needs to guide us, and to guide those who claim to represent us.

Now I clearly understand the emotion behind the desire to eliminate guns, especially from those who have lost loved ones at the point of a firearm. Even so, it is important to separate our emotions from logic and fact, because when we let emotions be the sole guide for decision-making, we often end up perpetuating the problem we are trying to solve. As a matter of fact, many of our current government programs are the result of emotional and politicized responses that, in practice, are contrary to logic and human nature. They exacerbate the very problem they are supposed to solve. When it comes to gun control, there simply is no logic to support the view that keeping the law abiding from owning guns will reduce crime.

The best and only way to handle crimes committed with firearms is to create strong deterrents and to do our best to capture and punish the abusers. In the final analysis, if we want the right to bear arms, we must accept the fact that someone may use a gun to take advantage of us.

Illegal Drug Use

Let's move on to illegal drug use and apply the same questions about how to deal with this abuse of freedom. Do our current drug laws take away freedoms or do they punish the abuse of freedom? I believe the answer is obvious. Here is the important question though; if someone ingests drugs while in their own home, and they somehow manage not to hurt or infringe upon the rights of anyone else, how can this be considered a crime?

There are two reasons this would make sense:

1) The belief that someone under the influence of drugs has a greater potential to harm another. Or;

2) That doing drugs is damaging to one's health so therefore it should be stopped.

Let's deal with these ideas one at a time:

First of all, the idea that someone has a greater potential to harm someone else while on drugs is simply irrelevant. We should not be in the business of punishing people for "potential" crimes. That is the stuff of movies, not free society. Somehow, we managed to get it right with alcohol, and as such, we do not take away the right to consume it, and we do not punish people for doing so, unless their actions directly harm's other people in some way. In other words, we trust our citizens to make the right choice, and we do not take away their rights until they make an inherently bad decision.

So why is this idea acceptable with alcohol but we have thousands of people in jail for use of a similar substance -- marijuana? It really does not make much sense unless the government has decided it can no longer trust its citizens.

Now, the idea that we should limit or ban drug use on account of the potential health hazards -- don't these hazards exist for alcohol? How many people are dying every year due to alcoholism and other health issues associated with drinking? Even so, somehow the right to drink remains. Again, I fail to see the difference between alcohol and some other illegal "drugs". Furthermore, since when do we believe that the inalienable right to pursue life, liberty, and happiness really means that we can only pursue healthy activities as mandated by law? We have the right to slowly kill ourselves in the pursuit of happiness and the government does not have the authority to take that away -- or at least they should not. Again, it boils down to trust. Later I will discuss in detail what rights the government does have verses the rights they claim to have. The difference between the two is considerable.

Let me take a moment and clarify that I am NOT in support of people breaking laws when they do not agree with them. Anyone who is presently in prison for drug use or selling drugs deserves to be there for not obeying the law of the land and it needs to remain that way until the laws are changed. And they need to change. Also, as a recovering addict, I feel the need to point out that I am not in favor of drug use in any way, shape, or form. People that get involved in drugs are making very poor choices that will adversely affect the balance of their lives and hurt the people they love. Believe me. I know. Nevertheless, remember, the job of government is to protect rights, not to protect people from themselves.

One thing we need to spend more time on in this culture is thinking about the difference between treatment and punishment. If a person has an addiction, does it really make sense to punish them for it? Does that person get any better by having a conviction on their record, or going through the hell that must be a prison sentence? Or does it make more sense to work with them and do our best to support them in making more healthy personal choices? To teach them about consequences. To give them access to the benefits of society that people on the fringe, like addicts, rarely get to see. It seems pretty obvious to me.

In the meantime, think about how many tax dollars could be saved if we limited our drug enforcement efforts to those people who infringe upon the rights of others with their drug use, instead of trying to take away the right from everyone. How many citizens would be out of prison and would not have a drug conviction on their record that kept them from progressing further in life? Think of what we could have done with all those billions of tax dollars wasted in our war on drugs like maintaining and improving this country's infrastructure, or not running budgets with huge deficits, or improving people's lives by reducing the tax burden for all citizens, maybe we could even have eliminated phrases like "unfunded mandates" or "bankrupt state government".

As an aside, I believe it is important to note that there is a huge difference between what our government can do and what an employer can do. Businesses can and should screen for drug use in their hiring practices. Why not? Just as it should be your right to consume drugs, it is a company's right to deny employment to you if you do so. Businesses and business owners have rights too.

The Health Police

Another growing trend in government is the belief that it is the role of government to ensure that you are physically healthy. Many cities around the country have already begun to ban "Trans Fats" and even fast food restaurants in some cases. It is all done in the name of protecting you from your own decisions. Once again, does this sound like the ability to pursue life, liberty, and happiness? Hardly! Unless the government can prove that your unhealthy actions have a direct impact on someone else's rights, then the government has no authority whatsoever to tell you what you can put in your face.

A common argument in favor of these types of health controls is that unhealthy eating is putting an undue burden upon social health programs. Therefore, what you eat falls under the domain of the public interest. As I will detail later in this book, this is an argument FOR basic universal health care for all. Think about it; If over the course of our entire lives, we had access to regular checkups, qualified doctors and specialists (like dietitians) and up to date health information without dealing with the bureaucracy of HMO's we would all live longer healthier lives. Unlike today, when so many of us did not have access to a decent insurance program and as a result of lack of early detection or failing health become a burden on society.

Reforming Criminals

The discussion of how we treat those who abuse the law is of the highest importance in a discussion about the cost of freedom. Criminals are a price we are all forced to pay for -- in the capture, prosecution, housing, and reintegration of them into our society.

It goes without saying that our current system of incarceration does very little to reform anyone. I would even go so far as to say that the current system does just the opposite. Prison has become a badge of honor for gang members and a training ground for the common criminal. Within prison walls, inmates get ahead through committing more crime and by assuming a gangster type mentality. When inmates are finally released into society, they are at a greater disadvantage than when they were first incarcerated due to the fact they are hampered by a criminal history. and have gained no real work or life experience. For this reason, I believe that we need a wholesale overhaul of the incarceration system that would require prison life to mirror that of real life.

How does a person get ahead in the real world? The answer is through hard work and education! In prison, it is the complete opposite. In the real world, you do not eat, and you do not get a place to live if you do not perform. In prison, these things are offered without price and the cost is passed on to the taxpayer. How does this practice help reform an inmate to society? It does not! Here is a different solution that might actually transform the criminals in our society, or at least ensure that they are not released if they are unable to change.

Every inmate should be required to pay the price for his or her daily sustenance through work. It does not matter if this work is productive or not. It could be digging holes and filling them back up again if that's what it takes. When an inmate receives a prison sentence there should be two phases to ensure full restitution to society. The first phase is the punishment phase. This is the mandatory time that must be served. The second phase is to assume the financial burden -- essentially having the inmate cover the cost of their incarceration. The inmate would not be available for parole until both phases were completed.

Now I recognize that there is no way for an inmate to cover the actual cost of their incarceration and that is not what I am suggesting. Instead, I propose that an inmate be paid credits for work performed that would be applied to the debt. You could use monopoly money if that's all that is available. If the cost to house the candidate were set at $20.00 per day then the inmate would have to earn a minimum of 20 credits of labor in order to pay that cost. If they do not perform well, then they receive fewer credits, thus pushing back their release date. The simple implementation of this plan would immediately require inmates to operate on the same level as those of us law-abiding citizens on the outside. However, I would not stop with basic pay for basic labor.

In the real world, you do not start out making a decent wage, and you do not start out having everything you want or need. Instead, we have to work our way up to these benefits. It should be no different with prison life. When an inmate arrives, they should receive the bare minimum in accommodations and should only be able to make the bare minimum as a wage. As time goes on, and as they show a good work ethic, and complete their work properly, they would have the opportunity to receive promotions and work that may be more fulfilling or that can help them build real life work experience. An inmate could feasibly pay off their financial burden early through hard work and promotions. This would in turn prepare them to function properly in society.

I have never been a fan of giving inmates free education in prison when the rest of us have to pay for it. Instead, if an inmate wants an education or to learn a trade, they should have to earn the credits to pay for it and they should have to attend night school after a full day of work. Nothing of value or benefit should be provided without a work requirement -- and I mean nothing. If an inmate wants access to magazines or television, they would have to work to a degree where they could have enough credits to pay for it. Possibly, they could even have access to a better food menu available to those who work harder and earn more. Any benefits that could be provided as a result of hard work and effort would be a great motivator in this environment.

When an inmate acts up or chooses not to follow the rules, they would be required to pay a fine, much like a speeding ticket. This would increase the financial portion of their sentence and in turn increase the amount of time before their release. For good behavior they could work towards bonuses and other amenities that would motivate them to greater success -- once again, mirroring the real world.

With a system like this in place, no prisoner would be released without having demonstrated the required ability to report to work on time, put in a hard day's work, and even exceed minimal requirements in order to get ahead. I believe that in this case employers would be more likely to hire parolees. I also believe that people who have spent time in prison would be less likely to return because they would know how much work and effort is constantly required to get out. More importantly, by the very nature of their release, they have learned how to function properly in society. Those inmates that are unwilling to live according to the rules of society would remain in prison indefinitely. Now this is a system that has a chance to truly reform criminals. It's called life.

Summary

We must ensure every enacted law deals strictly with those who abuse their rights. This is in contrast to minimizing or removing the rights of those who have done nothing wrong. One cost of freedom is that there are those who will abuse that freedom. Are you prepared to pay that cost? Do you understand that the purpose of government is to protect freedoms not lives? If so, then are you prepared to hold your representatives accountable to these principles? The idea of holding politicians accountable is another cost of freedom that will be covered in a later chapter.

2.
THE COST OF INTRUSIVE GOVERNMENT

"History affords us many instances of the ruin of states, by the prosecution of measures ill-suited to the temper and genius of their people. The ordaining of laws in favor of one part of the nation, to the prejudice and oppression of another, is certainly the most erroneous and mistaken policy. An equal dispensation of protection, rights, privileges, and advantages, is what every part is entitled to, and ought to enjoy... These measures never fail to create great and violent jealousies and animosities between the people favored and the people oppressed; whence a total separation of affections, interests, political obligations, and all manner of connections, by which the whole state is weakened".

~Benjamin Franklin, Emblematical Representations, Circa 1774

As I sit and listen to candidates at the federal, state, and local levels, it seems as though all I hear are promises about what the government can do for us. It's as if the role of government has shifted from its original form into a charitable organization that can solve every woe and can write a check for every problem. Should this be considered the proper role of government? I would suggest that it is just the opposite. This is why I believe that a basic cost of freedom is that our government must remain small, and have limited powers in reaching into our lives. I look at this as a "cost" because it means that sometimes we will have to sacrifice those benefits that our government could provide with the understanding that a government cannot provide anything to one group without taking from another.

The founders knew this concept well, and they hoped to create a government with limited powers that would serve only the basic needs of the people and nothing more while ensuring the freedom and opportunity to provide for our communities and ourselves. As I said before, this philosophy means that in order for the government to provide specific services it must take something from its citizens in order for it to be able provide it to everyone equally. Like taxes. Now you may genuinely believe that having our government do these things is a perfectly acceptable practice, but I would like you to consider several factors before you close your mind completely on this issue.

The Federal Government is Operating Outside of its Authority:

The first obstacle to the idea that it is the federal government's job to provide all kinds of specialized services is that the government has no Constitutional authority to do much of what it does -- and that includes most of what the politicians are promising. Instead, all that matters is that the idea sounds good. Well, if the government can do anything that simply sounds good, then of what value is our founding document? We must remember that the Constitution was designed to limit government, not to limit people. Anytime we simply let our representatives look past their own constraints, the Constitution loses strength and power.

How ironic is it that the party that claims to be all about Constitutional civil rights is the party that has no problem bypassing the Constitution in seeking more and more social programs outside of their authority? In addition, I would like to point out that the other side of the political aisle has not done well in resisting this temptation either. In practice, neither political party cares too much about the idea of proper Constitutional authority.

Our representatives only follow the Constitution when it is convenient to their political needs. The rest of the time, they simply pay lip service to it hoping that no one will notice. They rely on the people's ignorance of the Constitution as to how our government is supposed to work. Thus, the true fault lies with us, the voting public. We need to be educated in order to combat the ignorance that perpetuates the expansion of government and limits our precious freedoms. That's right -- an enlarged government will always equal fewer freedoms. This is an absolute truth in society that we must all learn and understand.

We are supposed to be able to rely on the Supreme Court to hold the legislature in check when they exceed their authority. But the court has clearly shown that as long as the idea sounds good, or matches their own political philosophy, then the Constitution can be overlooked. The courts exceed their authority by writing law instead of interpreting it. Thus, the final check and balance against a corrupt government must be the people themselves. However, we're so wrapped up in celebrity distractions and listening to what sounds good, that we are failing to see the damage that has been done and will be done as we drift farther away from the original intent.

Once again, the Constitution is designed to limit government, not the people. Article 1 Section 8 of the Constitution clearly states the authority of the United States Congress. In case you have not seen it for a while, here is what it says:

Article 1
Section 8 - Powers of Congress
~ The Congress shall have Power To lay and collect Taxes, Duties, Imposts and Excises, to pay the Debts and provide for the common Defense and general Welfare of the United States; but all Duties, Imposts and Excises shall be uniform throughout the United States;
~ To borrow money on the credit of the United States
~ To regulate Commerce with foreign Nations, and among the several States, and with the Indian Tribes;
~ To establish an uniform Rule of Naturalization, and uniform Laws on the subject of Bankruptcies throughout the United States;
~ To coin Money, regulate the Value thereof, and of foreign Coin, and fix the Standard of Weights and Measures;
~ To provide for the Punishment of counterfeiting the Securities and current Coin of the United States;
~ To establish Post Offices and Post Roads;
~ To promote the Progress of Science and useful Arts, by securing for limited Times to Authors and Inventors the exclusive Right to their respective Writings and Discoveries;
~ To constitute Tribunals inferior to the Supreme Court;
~ To define and punish Piracies and Felonies committed on the high Seas, and Offenses against the Law of Nations;
~ To declare War, grant Letters of Marque and Reprisal, and make Rules concerning Captures on Land and Water;

~ To raise and support Armies, but no Appropriation of Money to that Use shall be for a longer Term than two Years;

~ To provide and maintain a Navy;

~ To make Rules for the Government and Regulation of the land and naval Forces;

~ To provide for calling forth the Militia to execute the Laws of the Union, suppress Insurrections and repel Invasions;

~ To provide for organizing, arming, and disciplining the Militia, and for governing such Part of them as may be employed in the Service of the United States, reserving to the States respectively, the Appointment of the Officers, and the Authority of training the Militia according to the discipline prescribed by Congress;

~ To exercise exclusive Legislation in all Cases whatsoever, over such District (not exceeding ten Miles square) as may, by Cession of particular States, and the acceptance of Congress, become the Seat of the Government of the United States, and to exercise like Authority over All Places purchased by the Consent of the Legislature of the State in which the Same shall be, for the Erection of Forts, Magazines, Arsenals, dock-Yards, and other needful Buildings; And

~ To make all Laws which shall be necessary and proper for carrying into Execution the foregoing Powers, and all other Powers vested by this Constitution in the Government of the United States, or in any Department or Officer thereof.

Please take a moment and find for me in this section of the Constitution the authority of congress to force money out of people's paychecks in order to pay for the retirement of others. Show me where it says that the Federal government can tell the states how to educate their children. What about Medicare? What about universal health care? I could go on and on, but the truth is that the federal government is and has been operating outside of its stated authority for many years, and those seeking election today are promising even more unconstitutional programs and benefits.

Now I'm not suggesting that we abolish Social Security or give up on universal health care. So many of our citizens are about to retire based upon this great promise that it would be unthinkable to do so. Nevertheless, we can, and should, fix the problem by amending the Constitution to provide for such a program and a few basic others like health care.

Again, the point is that congress is clearly reaching outside the authority they were originally granted by the Constitution. However, the constitution was created to be a living document. It was designed to be updated as new technology became available, new priorities were defined by the people, and new realities changed our lives. Change is a powerful thing.

Unfortunately, those who seek to be our President continue to suggest that we stray further and further outside of these powers without addressing and maintaining our core philosophy. When we bypass the Constitution, it makes the document increasingly less relevant, and takes away the key organizing framework of our society. In its place, we have nothing but politically motivated rhetoric. This cannot be good and our founding fathers knew it -- which is why the tenth amendment in the Bill of Rights sought to clarify the Constitutional authority of the federal government:

- Amendment 10

The powers not delegated to the United States by the Constitution, nor prohibited by it to the States, are reserved to the States respectively, or to the People.

The tenth amendment clearly states that if the authority is not specifically delegated to the federal government then that power is reserved to the states, or to the people. This is for a very important reason -- once the federal government takes something over, it is next to impossible for the individuals of a state to have any future effect on that program. If the program is left at a state level, the chances are much better that any changes required by the will of the people will be achievable. After all, who knows better about the specific needs of its citizens? The federal government or those people that actually live and work in the state and communities in question? The federal government should only do those things that the federal government has been authorized to do as described in the Constitution. The rest of the work is best reserved for the states. The main problem is most of the States are broke! This is a direct result of the federal government overreaching its authority. Let me explain:

I'm really not sure at all why people believe that the federal government can do things better than the states or, under scrutiny, the private sector. All it takes is one look at most federal programs to understand that these federal organizations fail to meet their stated goals and do so by spending an enormous amount of money. In almost every case, the States could accomplish the task with more efficiency and at a smaller expense.

"It would reduce the whole instrument to a single phrase that of instituting a Congress with power to do whatever would be for the good of the United States; and as they would be the sole judges of the good or evil, it would be also a power to do whatever evil they please. Certainly no such universal power was meant to be given them. It [the Constitution] was intended to lace them up straightly within the enumerated powers and those without which, as means these powers could not be carried into effect

~ Thomas Jefferson, Opinion on a National Bank, February 15, 1791

A perfect example of this erroneous idea that the federal government should be involved in everything came shortly after the terrorist attacks of September 11, 2001. We were told that the airport screeners needed to be controlled and run by the federal government in order to avert future attacks. The problem was that there were no security breaches by airport screeners on September 11. They all did exactly what they were supposed to do. So why was there a rush to federalize airport screeners, instead of changing the guidelines to eliminate the items used to hijack the planes? So our representatives and our president could take the opportunity to expand its authority over the States and its citizens. We allowed our government to create one more gigantic, slow moving bureaucracy; Homeland Security, when all they needed to do was change the rules to eliminate box cutters and similar items from being allowed onto aircraft. Brilliant!

On top of that, by assuming this expanded responsibility as a way of convincing the population that the government was trying to make us safe, it then passed legislation that took away an unprecedented number of our Rights and Freedoms. And we let them do it. Instead of insisting the government find and punish the terrorists who committed this atrocity, the politicians used this situation to solidify federal authority and weaken State power. Ultimately becoming political terrorists themselves.

One of the ways that the United States has overstepped its power without technically violating the Constitution is by telling the states that if they expect to receive federal funds then they must comply with "Federal Guidelines." This way the Feds can say, "We're not forcing anyone to do anything -- therefore, we're not in direct violation of the separation of powers in the Constitution."

But remember, the Constitution only gives congress the authority to collect taxes for the programs that it has authority over. So how is it that they can collect taxes from us, and then tell us that we cannot have them back unless we comply, when they don't have the stated authority to butt their noses in where it doesn't belong in the first place? We should not be paying them taxes for something that they do not have the authority to do. Therefore, anytime you hear the government saying that they will only provide money if the state operates in a certain way, this is code for saying that they know that they don't have the authority to do this, but they think they've found a loop hole -- so they're just going to do it anyway. In my opinion, we should make a list of all the millions of dollars that are received by a state from the federal government for these types of programs, and then turn around and submit a bill to the federal government for an equal amount, as it is unlawful taxation. Congress and the office of the president are violating the law, and we, the American public, are standing by and letting them do it. Minimal amounts of these taxes should leave the states in the first place.

A wise and frugal government, which shall restrain men from injuring one another, which shall leave them otherwise free to regulate their own pursuits of industry and improvement, and shall not take from the mouth of labor the bread it has earned. This is the sum of good government, and this is necessary to close the circle of our felicity.

~ Thomas Jefferson, First Inaugural Address March 1801

There is No Money to do any of it!

It's one thing to collect taxes and then hold them over the states heads like an extortionist, but it is entirely another to continue to create new programs when there just is not any money to pay for them. Who gets to simply go out and spend money they do not have without serious repercussions down the road? Can it really be considered responsible to suggest even more entitlements when we are having problems funding the programs already in place? We must consider the fact that our current programs are outdated, failing or obsolete before we create even more financial problems for the generations to come.

What the congress is doing now in terms of managing the budget seems very much like the way Enron ran its organization. The head guys at Enron used an accounting practice called the "mark-to-market" method. This system allowed a company to book not only actual profits and losses incurred during a reporting period, but also "potential" future profits on deals closed in the same period. Including estimated pricing increases and adjusted profit margins! This is in essence making things up as they went along to meet analysts' predictions for growth. We are doing basically the same thing with government spending. By running huge deficits and taking the shortfalls from social security, we are in effect saying that our kids and grandchildren, maybe even our great grandchildren, will pay the bill for us. We're spending money no one has made yet!

Why don't we have someone who wants to be President who says that instead of creating new programs they're going to cut spending and restructure the tax code in order to pay down the debt? Certainly, that would have a profound effect on the lives of American citizens. If we had a President who really cared about the long-term health of the nation, the very first thing he/she would do is create a Presidential Committee whose sole purpose would be to review every Federal Program in existence and determine several factors:

1) Is the program Federal under the Constitution or should it be reserved to the states?

2) Is the program accomplishing the stated goal?

3) Is the program operating efficiently in terms of both manpower and expense?

4) Should the program be terminated?

Any President who would commit to this wholesale overhaul of our government would have my vote and in my estimation would generate more of a legacy than anyone focusing on foreign affairs, domestic policies, new entitlements, etc. After this review of government programs, the President should then focus his attention on legislation and court rulings that are made without proper authority.

"I think we have more machinery of government than is necessary, too many parasites living on the labor of the industrious."

~*Thomas Jefferson, letter to William Ludlow, September 6, 1824*

Unequal Taxation

As we know from our history lessons, one of the primary reasons that the founding fathers went to war was due to taxation without representation. Today our current tax code is considered only a source of mild frustration for most Americans. It currently has not created the same outrage that King George did simply because of the way it is structured. Most Americans today do not need to spend much time thinking about their taxes. We have franchised accounting firms and tax preparation software that will do the hard work for us. And many Americans look forward to getting an income tax refund every year and therefore view the IRS positively. But I believe that if the public knew a few things regarding the operations, structure and legality of this agency, they would wonder how it came to be and why for almost 100 years we have allowed the government to take a part of our income it was never authorized to collect. Such as:

1) The way the IRS currently assess taxes upon individuals is expressly prohibited by the constitution. The constitution allows the federal government to lay and impose taxes upon the population for specific purposes and only in a manner defined as "either direct or apportioned". "Direct" taxes are specific taxes such as the fee a person pays to buy a fishing license or the tax on a pack of cigarettes. If a person wishes to avoid these taxes, they do not go fishing or smoke. An "apportioned" tax means the government must impose the tax equally across all of the states such as the .009% gasoline tax we all pay when we fill our tanks.

2) The United States Supreme Court has on two prior occasions declared taxation on personal income at the federal level unconstitutional. The states do have the right to impose taxes on individual income and are unrestricted in how they choose to structure them. This is another reason why the states are the appropriate place to run most of the programs currently under federal authority.

3) Our current income tax laws were never ratified by the states in the manner defined in the constitution and therefore American citizens are paying money to the government it has no legal standing to collect. This is a fact. Most people think this is one of those "kook" ideas but I stand by this statement. To make it interesting, I'm offering this challenge; If someone can provide me with a copy of the actual law, written down and legally binding, granting the federal government with extra-constitutional powers giving it the right to tax personal income, I will pay them $100 cash. I feel pretty safe in making this offer since the group "Americans for Tax Reform" has been offering a $50,000 award for the same information for over 15 years. Several people, including former IRS employees, tax scholars, regular folks like you and I have attempted to collect this money and have not been successful.

4) The way our government structured the federal withholding laws created a willingness in the population to overlook all of these issues. As part of the revised payroll laws passed in the 1940's, most taxes are taken directly from a person's paycheck before the money becomes "real" to them. If American citizens collected that portion of their paycheck as regular income before receiving their tax bill, and then had to manage their cash flow and expenses in order to pay the annual tax bill by the deadline, Americans would have a far different opinion of the IRS. In fact, the government realized between 1913 (the year the current Federal Internal Revenue program was declared law), and 1944 (the year congress passed the revised federal payroll withholding laws) that they had a public relations nightmare on their hands. People hated the IRS. The congress and the administration had been looking at various ways to minimize the impact on the average American family for years before this option was finally approved.

Remember, this is money you earned through your labor or skills. It belongs to you. Our government withholds it from you for the stated purpose of funding the day-to-day activities of various programs run by the federal government, investing in improvements, completing maintenance and upgrading the basic infrastructure of our country, including paying the expenses related to our foreign policies. But if this were the case, why are we running huge deficits? Why is social security on the verge of going bankrupt? Why do we not have enough tax revenue coming in to cover the cost of doing business? I will answer these questions in a later chapter.

By deducting the federal tax from a person's paycheck, the government has created a false perception in the minds of Americans. The government attempted to calculate the math used so the amount deducted from a person's paycheck is set so that average worker either breaks even or gets a refund check. By assessing taxes in this manner, the government changed how Americans viewed the IRS. People used to dread the tax deadline and viewed the IRS with suspicion and anger. Today, if people think of the IRS at all it is mostly in a positive light as the agency that sends them a check once a year. This is pure manipulation of the American people. They are taking money from us illegally and most of us never give it a second thought.

What most people fail to realize is the government is taking a share of the money you earned in an illegal manner to use for unconstitutional programs. Think about that. This should make you mad. What makes this even worse is that through the mismanagement of that same government these programs are going broke anyway. If the average American were to look at the percentage of their paycheck that is deducted for federal withholding and compare that to the size of their IRS tax return, they would start looking for large quantities of tea and a harbor to toss it into.

Does anyone believe for a single second that our founders envisioned a system that even those who enforce it cannot understand? Can anyone say that we have taxation with representation today? Not if most Americans do not know what is going on. Those who claim to represent us seem to think that our income is the government's to keep, and that we should feel fortunate to retain a smaller and smaller percentage of what we earn.

Even more disturbing than the idea that 'we the people' continue to allow a program to operate that few of us agree with is, that the current tax code is illegal under the 14th amendment, which requires that every citizen receive equal protection under the law. Since the tax code is a law that is forced upon all citizens, it must be equal under this amendment – but is it? Can a code that holds people to different tax percentages based upon income levels, marital status or deductible expenses be considered equal? The only answer is that it cannot! If one citizen is required to pay 15% then every citizen must pay that same percentage, regardless of income or financial status. This is the only system that can be considered "equal." If our current representatives feel the need to have unequal protection regarding the tax law then they must amend the 14th amendment. Allowing them to simply look past it is allowing the integrity of this document to be greatly diminished.

I have never quite understood why this tax code is allowed to stand as it is. I watch organizations like the ACLU that claim to be fighting for our civil liberties, yet when it comes to taxation and unconstitutional social programs they remain completely silent. I believe that this silence reveals a political agenda on their part. Of course, they would deny it, but how else can it be explained that in their fight to protect rights they fail to protect the integrity of the Constitution when it comes to fiscal matters? We hear them talk about free speech and separation of church and state, yet we never hear them battle the government for overreaching its authority on entitlement programs. You have to wonder why this is.

The Right to Keep What You Earn

As I mentioned before, there is one political party that has set themselves up as the standard-bearers for Civil Rights and another party that claims to be the standard-bearer of fiscal responsibility. What I do not understand is how these same parties have no problem taking away your right to keep what you earn. That's correct -- I said "your right" to keep what you earn. They seem to believe that they should be allowed access to all of our money for the needs of others, and that we should all feel grateful that they let us keep anything at all.

We have let the idea creep into our society that we all need to give back, or that we need to spread the wealth. This implies that we are where we are because we took from others. But we did not take, we earned what we have, and this needs to be remembered by us and by our government. We should not be made to feel guilty because we have amassed wealth or have achieved a level in life where we make a respectable wage. As long as you have earned it, or inherited it legally, then it belongs to you. No one in the government has a right to tell you that you now need to sacrifice or give your money to them, so they can redistribute it. If you want to give of your financial means, then I encourage you to do so, but you should not be compelled to do so while others pay nothing at all. If you are asking where the right to keep what you earn is listed in the Constitution, then I am afraid that you do not understand the Constitution. Remember, this document was designed to limit the government, not the people. Our rights are not limited by the Constitution -- in fact, it is just the opposite. This guarantee is driven home in the 9th amendment, which reads-

Amendment 9

The enumeration in the Constitution, of certain rights, shall not be construed to deny or disparage others retained by the people.

This amendment says that just because the founders took the time to single out certain rights that it does not mean that these are our only rights. Money is your property! You earned it and the federal government does not have the authority to take it in order to give it to other people. The federal government is strictly regulated by our founding document and the government needs to get back to strict accountability to the Constitution.

We must remember one thing of paramount importance: --- That the U.S. government is nothing more than the people granting certain authority to elected representatives to make decisions for the common good --- That's it. The government is not a body of people with the authority to tell people how to live or how much of their own money they can keep. We agree to pay taxes for certain goods and services that benefit the whole, and for much of the history of the United States there was no federal tax. Taking money from one person to give to another person, cause, or company, in the form of grants, goods or services is not within their lawful authority, nor is it just, or fair.

To many of you this may sound like the height of selfishness. But, please do not misunderstand, I cannot find words strong enough to convey how I feel about giving back. I have personally benefited by receiving assistance from both government agencies and private non-profit organizations in my life. As someone who has benefited personally, I rigidly adhere to a policy of making sure that I return the favor. We should absolutely help one another with our time, talents, and means. But we should not be constrained to do so. As I will explain later in this book, there is a considerable difference between an individual trying to help others voluntarily, and the same individual being forced to help by the government.

In our current tax system, we give away a huge part of our earnings to feed a politicized set of institutions that mishandle and over-spend our money. Then, without being required to fix anything, they have the audacity to ask for more money. Our politicians do not even take into consideration how many of the institutions themselves need to be leaner and become better stewards of our tax dollars. These programs waste our money and then expect to get more. They act like spoiled teenagers more than responsible entities that are supposed to be staffed with professionals we can trust. We have come to simply accept this reality. It is not only unfair and not supported by the Constitution; it is also increasingly putting us at an economic disadvantage in a global marketplace and destroying our credibility.

"The ordaining of laws in favor of one part of the nation, to the prejudice and oppression of another, is certainly the most erroneous and mistaken policy. An equal dispensation of protection, rights, privileges, and advantages, is what every part is entitled to, and ought to enjoy."

~ Benjamin Franklin, Emblematical Representations, Circa 1774

Abortion

There is no need to look any further than the federal government's interference with abortion to see how the Constitution is no longer in play. Can anyone find any statement within the Constitution to justify the Supreme Court's decision with Roe vs. Wade? The authority for the Supreme Court to rule in any manner on this subject does not exist. They created law where there was none -- which is not within their authority to do, and the nation just accepted the decision without issue.

The truth is abortion is an issue for the states, not the federal government, since the Constitution does not provide the authority for Congress, or the President, or the Supreme Court to get involved. This battle should be fought on a state level, and in that situation, I am sure that we would have states that allow the procedure and states that would elect to make the procedure illegal. The battle would be fought on a local level and not the federal level, where citizens have little or no impact. And, once again, I will point out, if those in the federal government feel that it is so important for the federal government to get involved with important issues such as this then they should be required to amend the Constitution to provide for this authority.

While on the subject of abortion, let me just provide a few personal beliefs regarding this subject. First, It bothers me greatly that those in favor of the right to choose call their movement the "Pro-Choice" movement. I think it would be better termed the "Pro-Reckless Behavior" movement or the "Pro-Irresponsibility" movement. Later in this book, I will discuss the importance of natural consequences in greater detail, but suffice to say here that the "Pro-Choice" movement simply wants to avoid the consequences of choice. After all, last time I checked, it takes a number of choices to conceive a child; the choice to be sexually active, the choice to do so unprotected, and then finally, the choice to end the life of an unborn fetus. Pregnancy is always a choice unless it involves rape or incest. Always! And choices have consequences. It used to be that if you did not want to face the consequences that you would make a responsible choice. But not today! Today we strive for the ability to make any reckless choice we want and to remove the consequences to the point of medical procedures. If you do not like the consequences, make a better choice! How is that for a political movement?

Second, I am also bothered that their opposition calls themselves the "Pro-Life" movement. A better name for this group might be the "Pro-Limitation of Freedom" movement or "Pro-Impose our Beliefs on Others" movement. I believe that this country was founded on the concepts of self-determination and individual freedom. As such, if something is legal, a person should not have to be harassed for, or concerned for their safety by, engaging in that activity. I support anyone who has strong beliefs on important issues and makes their opinions known, even if I disagree with those opinions. That is what I consider good citizenship. But as soon as someone crosses the line where they decide to take away another person's ability to make their own decisions, we need to step in. If someone, or some couple, were to be forced to have a baby that they are unprepared for, or incapable of taking care of, what kind of life are we condemning that child to live? What fate are we forcing the parents to accept? In addition, what gives us the right to try to force someone to live by the ideals and belief systems we choose to live by? Nothing. I saw a bumper sticker years ago that sums this up fairly well. It read: "If you don't trust me to make a choice, how can you trust me to raise a child?" The answer is- our opinion is irrelevant.

On a personal note, as I write this book, I am about to celebrate my 45th birthday. I am a former musician and bar owner, I have been a successful producer of both content for television and feature films. I live in southern California, and lived temporarily in places like Australia, England, Spain, Mexico and Thailand. I make enough money to live as comfortably as I choose. I am single today, but was married for a little over 7 years to a woman who was my best friend and then widowed. I have also been sexually active since I was thirteen. Yet, I have managed not to have any children nor have I, with any of my ex-girlfriends, found ourselves in the position where we needed to consider an abortion. How is that possible? By being responsible for the actions I take. It is that simple.

Now, having said all of that I want to go on record as stating that I am 100% for a woman having the ability to choose to have an abortion. My only wish is that they occurred much more rarely than they do. I believe a citizen's right of self-determination is fundamental. And that for any number of reasons a woman, or a couple, may decide that time or circumstances are not right for the huge commitment necessary in raising a child. I personally believe adoption would be a wonderful alternative in many of the situations that currently end in abortion. Additionally, I want people to assume more responsibility for the actions they take.

I find it unfortunate for our society that there are so many couples who are having such difficulty in conceiving a child that there are as many abortions occurring as there are today. More of an effort needs to be directed at bringing these two separate situations together.

One of the crazy things that occurs to me about the world we live in is the impact that one soul can have on the entire globe. By removing just a handful of key figures from our history, our entire existence changes completely. Diseases may not have been cured, technology may not have been invented, lives may not have been saved, and countries may not have been formed. How different would our world be if George Washington's mother had an abortion? What about Abraham Lincoln, Martin Luther King Jr., Winston Churchill, Gandhi, etc.? What if the cure for cancer lies within the mind of a fetus that was removed from a mother's womb? And yes, you could reverse the question and ask how different the world would be if the likes of Hitler or Genghis Khan, Napoleon or any of the other historical figures that caused wars or famine would have been aborted. It is an interesting moral question. There will always be good and evil in the world and 'we the people' will acknowledge the good and combat that evil whenever we find it. But so much of our shared history comes from the actions of that "one" person in a particular place and time. We really need to consider these and many more questions when deciding what choices we are going to make.

Regardless of how the government responds to abortion, I would appeal to you, at the most basic level, to really consider the action you take. That tissue inside of you has enormous potential for good, and it is a boy or a girl that is alive. Fundamentally, we feel and know this. There is no mother out there that does not feel the spirit of that unborn child, and if you listen close, enough you will hear its desire to live. Carry it for nine months and then give it to someone who can care for the child, but please do not make a decision that ends that life and potentially ruins yours. You will never regret bringing that life onto the earth. But you could be forever scarred by ending it.

Perhaps my biggest frustration within the law, both local and federal, is how we have now decided that if the fetus is wanted, then it is a life, but if it's not wanted, then it's just tissue that can be removed at will. For example, in the high profile case of Scott Peterson, he was convicted and sentenced for the killing of his wife and her unborn fetus -- that is two murders. Yet if Laci had wanted to, she could have gone down to an abortion clinic and had that tissue removed at any time, and it would have been considered legal. How did we get ourselves into a place where only if a fetus is wanted is it considered a life? It seems to me that either it is a life, protectable by the state, or it is not. The fact that the child was planned and wanted, or was unplanned and unwanted, should not enter the picture. Intellectually, I have wondered what would happen if there was ever a case where a pregnant woman was killed on the way to an abortion clinic. Would her killer be charged with one murder or two? After all, the fetus was not wanted, so therefore the killer should only be charged with one murder, right? How would the prosecution or the defense team handle this legal argument? How would the judge rule or the jury react? How can this logic be allowed to stand? Life is life, regardless of the context. Life should be protected!

<u>Hate Crimes</u>

We must understand that we cannot use laws to regulate ones emotions. We are not mind readers, nor does our government have the authority to control our thoughts.

But isn't that the exact goal of hate crimes legislation; to regulate an emotion, or thought, and suggest that crimes that stem from these types of thoughts deserve greater punishment than those that are born from other emotions? The problem is that in trying to protect those who are being discriminated against, and attacked based upon their race, sexual orientation or other difference, we are in turn discriminating against those who face similar attacks, but for different reasons. As much as people may think that this sounds like a good idea, the 14th amendment of the Constitution clearly requires that every citizen have equal protection under the law.

How can it be equal protection if the same type of assault occurs to two different people, but the motivation for one was greed, and the other was hate, so the attackers get two different sentences? Did the man who was assaulted for his wallet receive any less physical damage than the man who was assaulted because of his difference? Is hate a worse emotion than greed? Some may think so, but in saying that one crime of emotion carries a greater punishment, we are discriminating against the other – and the demands of justice are denied.

Every crime is born of some type of emotion, and many times, it is hatred. But not always hatred for someone based upon skin color or lifestyle. Instead, it may be hatred for the man who stole your girlfriend, or for the person who has a great deal of money. Is this hatred any less tolerable than hatred based upon color of skin?

Hate crime legislation says yes, but again, I would contend that this couldn't be considered equal protection under the law. Our laws should focus on the action, not the emotion. We should not allow ourselves to get into the mindset that one crime of emotion carries a greater punishment than the exact same crime born of a separate emotion. Crime is crime, and the punishments should be the same for the crime committed, if we are going to remain true to the principle of equality for all.

Justice is supposed to be blind. That's why Lady Justice is always portrayed wearing a blindfold. If we start looking into a person's heart

ERIC J. KISER

or soul before we assess the punishment for a crime, we should put her in a coffin as well, because true justice will be as good as dead.

Equality via Legislation

The history of our nation is a difficult one when it comes to civil rights. The United States was born out of a need for individual freedoms, yet at the same time, in an incredibly insensitive form of compromise, it denied these basic freedoms based upon the color of a person's skin. How could such greatness have emerged with such an evil practice included in the laws and daily actions of everyday life? Today, there are those who would discount the positive influences of this nation because of those sins in our early history. These same people would suggest that the work and accomplishments of our founding fathers is nullified by the fact that many of them owned slaves. As I've studied history and people in general, I've come to a belief that it is not proper, or just, to place our modern day understanding and enlightenment upon those who came before us; especially, hundreds of years before us. It was a very different time. Can we say with certainty that if we were born in those times, and brought up under the same beliefs and cultural norms, that somehow we would have acted differently?

Fortunately, there were many during these times that saw the error of this practice and fought against it. When assessing the history of our nation, I believe that it is critical to point out that the United States did not bring slavery to this continent, but it did eventually end it. Now the United States is seen as a civil rights champion throughout the globe. No, our history is not perfect, and yes, we could spend all day long focusing on where we have been, instead of how far we have come -- and where we are going. Through long fought conflicts on the battlefield, and in the legislature, we have finally come to a place where, at least on paper, all people are guaranteed those God given rights that were spoken of so long ago in the Declaration of Independence.

Anytime we are faced with a crisis, there is a danger of pursuing the issue with such aggression that we actually tip the scales to the other side, thus destroying the rights of others in the name of repairing the initial wrong? It is the use of the government in this fashion that I will speak to in this section. We must recognize that one of the costs of our freedom is that even though racism and discrimination still exist, we

40

cannot increase the size of government to repair all woes, or at least we cannot do so without taking away the rights of those who have done nothing wrong.

The government cannot end racism! I am sorry, but this is simply impossible! The only thing the government can, and should do, is ensure that every citizen has proper recourse when they are discriminated against for any reason. That's it! It is not against the law, nor should it ever be, to hate someone for any reason. If you want to hate someone because of his or her skin color, be my guest. If you want to hate someone because of his or her financial status, go ahead. Maybe they stole your girlfriend or that million-dollar idea you had. In some way or another, we all experience hate. Maybe you hate someone because their ancestors owned slaves. Should that hatred be eliminated by law as well? Absolutely not! One thing I have learned in my life is that if you look hard enough at anyone for a reason to hate him or her, you will find it, regardless of skin color. So, go ahead. Hate away! Let it fill your life, if you think it will do you any good. I hope that you will realize some day that hatred of any form or fashion can destroy your life. Meanwhile, the person or group to which all of your hatred was focused goes on oblivious to you, and your sad emotional state. The only person hate ultimately hurts is the possessor of it.

"If we can prevent the government from wasting the labors of the people, under the pretence of taking care of them, they must become happy."

~ Thomas Jefferson, letter to Thomas Cooper, Nov 29, 1802

Affirmative Action

Another place where government has sought to end discrimination by using discrimination, or to end racism with racism, is via the policy of Affirmative Action. Affirmative Action was created for an admirable purpose. To level the playing field and create opportunities for those who were not treated equal by society under an outdated frame of thinking. While you may not agree with the wording I use, we all understand that the nature of this system is to discriminate in favor of minorities in order to right the wrongs of the past.

Again, while this all sounds fine and good on paper, the idea of placing someone in a position using race as a primary factor should not be considered equal protection under the law. This is a clear case where former presidents of the United States, and the Courts, have overstepped their Constitutional powers in a big way. In essence, they are saying that the 14th amendment cannot apply to Affirmative Action because of the discrimination of the past. What gives these presidents and the Courts the authority to override the Constitution in this manner? Nothing! They believe this practice is acceptable, so the fact that the Constitution does not allow for it is not important. So, once again, how can anything in the Constitution be considered firm and binding? The truth is that the Constitution has become an inconvenience for our current and past representatives, unless our founding document happens to support their position. Otherwise, they just look past it for the "good of the people."

We cannot end racism with racism! We cannot end discrimination with discrimination. The mere act of placing one candidate over another because of his or her race is discrimination, and it is wrong because it punishes someone because of his or her skin color, whether that skin is black, white, brown, yellow, orange or green. This is exactly what we were trying to correct, isn't it?

Doesn't it also punish someone who most likely had nothing to do with the decisions and discriminations of the past? The belief that simply by changing the rules of the game, everyone will come out a winner, is just wrong. Life does not work that way. We are allowing the government to decide who will win and who will lose, based upon the color of their skin. I thought we were supposed to be past that.

I think what our legislature was trying to do was change what is in people's hearts and minds, and as we have discussed, that is an impossible task. What I think we should consider is not necessarily eliminating the practice of Affirmative Action, but revising these laws to reflect the natural course of what we wish to accomplish. How do you get people to change their minds or actions about a subject? Through positive experiences, education and changing social perspectives. I really believe that this has already been happening over the last few decades.

For hundreds, if not thousands, of years white people viewed themselves as superior to other races. It seems so obviously wrong today because advances in science have proven that we are all human beings

42

under the skin. We are 99.9% similar and only .01% different. But, back in the 1860's, people who believed the old way of thinking their entire lives were forced to accept a new reality because society changed the rules. I believe that expecting segments of society to accept these new rules overnight was an unrealistic expectation, just based on human nature. People may have gone along with the new rules in "polite society", but in the privacy of their homes and the recesses of their hearts, they clung to the beliefs they were raised on. And they raised their children to believe in the old rules.

This is the reason it took almost a hundred years to go from ending the evil practice of slavery to ending the 'Jim Crow' policies of the south. It took almost one hundred years for the generational shift to occur. Over that period of time, as black people were integrating themselves into society through hard work, strength of character and sheer determination, more and more white people had reason to interact with them on a personal or professional level. And the old belief systems and stereotypes, ever so slowly, began to melt away. By the 1950's, enough Americans had practical experience with black people as equals to learn, and come to believe, the fact that we are all equal beings. Put another way; through individual experiences, enough white people were educated to the point where social perspectives began to change.

It was during this period that society began to look at ways of creating equal opportunities in the areas of life where injustices still occurred. Hiring practices, college admissions, neighborhood housing covenants and many other obstacles were put in place as a means by which segments of society still engaged in discriminatory practices, even if they were not talked about. A 'good old boy' network still existed that limited the ability of all people of color to achieve the great promise of this country. So we passed Affirmative Action laws to create change. I believe this was probably the best action we could come up with at the time. And, for the most part, they have worked. But I also believe that as more time goes by these laws become less necessary because social attitudes continue to change. We should also be concerned that this law does not get the chance to institutionalize the practice of reverse discrimination. This is why I propose modifying these laws to allow for periodic reviews that can begin to reduce or eliminate these laws in the areas were they have done their job.

It is in everyone's best interest to see these laws go away. It means we have reached a point in society where we do not need their guidance anymore. Isn't that the goal we should all be working towards?

How to End Racism and Discrimination Today

How do you change a man's heart in this day and age? Certainly not with law! In fact, the only thing a law will do is make them more resolute in their hatred and anger! So, once the laws are equal, how do we go about convincing everyone that man should not be judged by the color of his skin, but instead, by the content of his character? The answer is in the showing of the content of one's character, not in more government laws and programs.

When Tiger Woods entered the golf world, there were still many golf organizations that wanted nothing to do with black players. He could have stood outside of these places with a picket sign, demanding entry, and fighting for laws to be passed that would allow him to play. Would that have done any good? Probably not! His solution was much different; if he becomes the best in the world, then no one would turn him away.

That is exactly what he did. In the process, he has opened what was once a very exclusive sport to a whole new demographic. There are those in these exclusive circles that bemoan his success, but there are many others that have gone through a sort of conversion; not only because of what a great player Tiger is, but also because of how he carries himself on and off the course. They have seen the content of his character, and have been changed by it. No law in the world could have achieved this accomplishment.

Take a look at almost every case where a minority has broken into a sport, or a high ranking job, or a political position, and you will find someone who became so good at what they do, that they simply could not be denied any longer. Many of these sports where blacks used to be banned are now dominated by black players. Their talents and abilities simply could not be overlooked. Yet every one of them could have stood outside of the stadium with a picket sign, or demanded new and greater Affirmative Action laws. After all, picketers did not open up professional baseball to black players; it was the character and talents of one Jackie Robinson. Thankfully, for whatever reason, these athletes felt as though their abilities would trump old stereotypes. They were right. Where would these sports be today if these players waited for the laws and the government to come to them instead of plowing forward against the odds?

If ever there could be a case made for Affirmative Action today, certainly it would be within the National Basketball Association, where over 80% of the players are black. If we allow the logic of many of the activists today, then we should compare the percentage of blacks in the NBA with the percentage of blacks in the larger society. Seeing how there is an over-representation of blacks in the NBA, racism must be involved. In this case, the racism would be against white people, correct? Can you imagine teams that were designed to have the right racial makeup instead of teams recruited based upon talent? We might as well throw out the score and make sure that each team gets equal wins throughout the year as well. The idea of Affirmative Action is just silly when we apply it to professional sports! The best players should play, regardless of their race, because the goal is to win. So why is it any different in the business world? After all, the NBA is a business! Aren't employers entitled to the best candidates regardless of racial makeup? Shouldn't they be able to recruit based upon talent and experience so they can win? The NBA is a perfect example of how talent can overcome adversity, stereotypes, and ignorance in a big way.

The rest of the private sector should be no different. As long as every citizen has access to proper recourse when problems occur, we should not allow our government to get involved beyond this, because when it does, by necessity, it implements discrimination and the loss of rights on behalf of one group or another. The same goes for access to education as well.

The Case Against Government Discrimination

Early in my career and again a few years later, while doing some consulting for a local business I was confronted with two completely different types of discrimination that taught me important lessons. My first example came a few years ago while I was helping a local firm hire and train new staff. As I had always done in the past, I put the applicants through the same screening process and eventually made job offers based upon whom I felt was most qualified, and able to properly fulfill the job requirements. After a brief training period, I was ready to put the new staff to work, and I was generally pleased with the results. On the last day of training, one of the company executives came to the classroom to inspect my progress and see how the new staff was progressing. After several minutes of watching, he called me over to where he was sitting with a very concerned look on his face.

"Who is that?" he asked, as he pointed to the individual that I considered being one of the best recruits. I explained that the person was one of the new hires, and that out of all of the new staff members, he was turning out to be one of the best. To my shock and amazement, the executive then explained to me, "We don't hire their kind here!" Honestly, at first I had no idea what he meant. This was 2004! "Certainly he was not talking about the fact that this guy was black," I thought to myself. "What do you mean "their kind"," I asked with a very puzzled tone. He then quietly said, "you know….we don't hire black people. We have never had good luck hiring African-Americans." I quickly explained to him that everyone who had been working with this particular recruit seemed to be very happy, and that in my opinion he was doing great. The executive then made it painfully clear to me that I was to fire him immediately and cease hiring his kind, or my services would not be needed any longer.

Needless to say, I was greatly troubled by this circumstance, and having to explain things to this bright young man was something that I did not want to do. How do you explain to someone that, after all their hard work and effort, the color of their skin is all that people see? Obviously, I gave notice and stopped working with that company. I hope that young man found a place where his skills and work ethic were valued over his skin color. I did encourage him to seek legal recourse, and told him that I would gladly help, but he said he did not want anything to do with them and just moved on.

The second occurrence with discrimination in the workplace happened early in my career. I had submitted my resume for a manager position to a multi-national corporation located in my town. This was a company that was considered the industry leader in its field, and was experiencing amazing growth at that time. The human resource person who set up the interview let me know that a large number of resumes had been sent in for this and every other opening the company had, and that I was fortunate to have been asked to come in for an interview. I did well, and received a call back to come in for a second round of interviews with the peers of whoever was offered the position would be working with every day. Again, I did well and thought that I had a very good chance of being offered the position.

After a week or so, I received a call with a formal job offer, but the offer was not for the job I had interviewed for. When I asked for clarification, I was told that they had offered the original position to someone else but were actually creating a position in the same department and offering it to me. This job was in effect "the second in command" to the position for which I had applied. I accepted the reduced position feeling that this was a chance for me to get my foot in the door with a great company. I was happy to go to work there.

Once I had started my new job one of the executives came down to our department and invited me to lunch. It was during this meeting that I got the full story of why I was offered the position. You see, I had been hired as the "assistant" manager because, due to the equal opportunity hiring practices of the company, HR. had determined that a minority needed to be placed in the position of manager. Therefore, they had chosen a black man that had worked with one of the other executives at a different company based on his referral. All of the people who had interviewed both of us had said they wanted to hire me for the position, but based on the law, HR. chose to hire the other candidate. The only problem was this man had not been a manager at his old company and did not have the experience needed to do the job. I'm not suggesting that he could not learn what he needed to learn. But the reason they suspected he would not do well in this role was the fact that this company was incredibly fast paced and had products that were taking over the market and couldn't be produced in enough quantities to fill all the orders. The job required a person who did not need to learn how to do something, but one that already had experience with unplanned growth and quick response planning. If this person had been given the job I was offered, he would have done great and could have grown into an outstanding manager over time. But he wasn't.

As it turned out, I was asked to do whatever it took to ensure the department functioned as needed while staying in the job I had taken. Over the next couple of weeks, an unspoken shift in roles occurred as the manager and I basically traded jobs, without trading titles or pay. I was making the decisions and he was doing the work. People began to recognize what was going on and coming to me with questions or requests as a matter of efficiency. I even typed up our departments weekly reports while sitting at his computer so they would be sent from his email account. Also, I would spend an hour bringing him up to speed on the issues and actions of "our" team before he would go into the staff meetings he had with his boss just so it would seem like he was doing his job. We accomplished what needed to be done but at great cost to the teams overall efficiency and moral. Much more time was spent than necessary in keeping up this facade. We went on like this for over a year. Finally, enough people in executive management learned of what was going on and this person was eventually transferred to another division in a non-management role, where he thrived. And I was promoted to "official" manager of the department.

The person who was hired to be manager told me later that his health had suffered from the stress he had been living with under the threat of being discovered. I was experiencing stress and frustrations watching someone else collect the pay and take the credit for my work product. It got so bad that I almost left the company to go work elsewhere. And the company suffered because it could have accomplished its goals sooner if it had been able to hire the right person in the first place.

This leads me to the point I am trying to make by sharing these stories with you. These are both excellent examples of everything that is wrong with discrimination in the work place and looking to quota systems as a solution. In the first story, we see the blind arrogance of some business executives to the times in which we live, and in the second story, we see the damage that can be done by looking to government to solve the problem. Everyone suffers as a result of trying to legislate equality.

I realize that the term Affirmative Action has different meanings for some. In its purest sense, it is nothing more than an effort to make sure that recruiting efforts or hiring practices are focused on all races, instead of just one or two. However, even in its purest sense Affirmative Action is not productive or proper. The goal should always be to hire the best employee for the job regardless of race. We should not get in the practice of looking at the racial makeup of companies or at anything that resembles a quota. This forces us to look at race instead of performance or experience or most important, the content of a person's character.

The Multi-Cultural Myth

As we discuss the issue of race relations in this country, I think it is of great importance to discuss the "new ideas" in our education system and other places that are designed to weed out racism. A common phrase that I've heard to describe these programs is "Multi-Cultural-ism." The idea is that if we bring students together and teach them about each other's culture and differences then magically they will not grow up as racists. As I have watched my friends' children go through this education, it almost feels as though the administrators believe that some parents are instilling their children with racist attitudes -- and that only through multiculturalism will they be able to reverse the damage that those parents have done. Once again, the idea of multi-cultural-ism sounds wonderful, but it goes against human nature entirely, and therefore, probably does more harm than good.

How do you choose your friends? How did you choose your spouse? Were you put in a large room and taught about what makes you different? Probably not! The truth is that human nature is to choose friends based upon commonality, not differences. I have a very diverse group of friends that I see on a regular basis because we have a common interest in politics. If it were not for this common ground, we probably would pass each other on the street without saying so much as hello. Politics brought us together, and along the way, we learned about our differences. This is why we have clubs and organizations that focus on commonalities instead of differences. Have you ever seen the "We are Different Club" or the "Nothing in Common Club?" They don't exist because it is human nature to be around people with whom we have commonalities -- and by the way, there is absolutely nothing wrong with this. It is not racist for a bunch of white people to hang out with each other because they have similar backgrounds and interest. The same goes for a group of African-Americans, Hispanics, etc... I can guarantee you that anytime you see a group of people together that have a diversified background that they came together based upon some common theme. That is how we work and it is nothing to be ashamed of.

From Multi-Cultural-ism to Uni-Culturalism

What if, instead of teaching our children about their differences, we instead focused on what makes us all the same? Instead of multiculturalism, we should have uni-culturalism, where we teach our children about this one nation that brings us together and gives us the freedoms we enjoy. Oddly enough, sometimes it feels like the American culture is the one culture that is always left out of multi-cultural instruction, and that is the one culture that we all have in common.

When it comes to civil rights, our government has done its job. Everyone has equal protection under the law. Does that mean that everyone is treated equally? Absolutely not! But this is a direct cost of a free society; that there will be those who do not get a fair shake, or that are falsely accused, or that face racism and discrimination in their lives. As I stated early on in this book, the solution in these circumstances is to seek ways to punish the abuser of freedom and to deter such abuse. Wide sweeping actions that punish everyone because of the sins of the few cannot be accepted. We should look at no man as a racist until he is proven to be such. We should look at no organization and assume discrimination because of racial makeup without evidence beyond that to support such claims. All men and women should be looked at as fine upstanding citizens, both in business and in their personal lives, until there is cause to think otherwise.

One thing I can tell you for sure is that if human beings are still alive and kicking 10,000 years from now, I doubt they will have this problem. By then, I believe we will be one big "mocha" colored community and the happier for it.

"Let us tenderly and kindly cherish, therefore, the means of knowledge. Let us dare to read, think, speak, and write."

~ *John Adams*

Education

There simply is no other way for me to say this; we are off our rocker when it comes to education today! I do not know exactly when we lost all logic and replaced it with emotion but we have. Our current system is failing our students and is failing our hard working teachers as well. The idea behind the "No Child Left Behind" Act seems to be a simple one; if we never leave, then no one will be left behind.

We are "dumbing" down standards and protecting our children from failure, and the natural consequences of life, and we have tied the hands of our teachers with national testing standards that do not match the local needs of the children.

The first thing to remember, as always, as we try and figure out what is wrong with our education system today, is that under the constitution our federal government has no authority over the states and the education they provide. So how do they get away with telling us what to do? I talked about it earlier in the book when I explained that they use federal tax dollars to extort what they need and want from public schools -- and if these schools do not comply, then they will not get these federal funds. Federal funds, I will say again, that should never have left the state in the first place. Remember that the Constitution only gives the federal government the authority to levy taxes for programs it has authority to initiate. But why let a little thing like the Constitution get in the way when it comes to the future of our children?

What makes the federal government believe they have a clue about how to educate our children! It blows my mind that the Courts, Congress and the President of the United States think they know the slightest thing about how to educate the children in your state or your city better than the local education professionals. It is time that the states stand up and tell the federal government to stop.

The Number One Factor in a Child's Education

Let's start with the most basic factor in a child's education. If I asked you what the most important factor is for a child to get a good education, what would your answer be? Would it be class size? How about spending per student? Maybe it's parental involvement? The truth may surprise you.

According to the testing data that I've seen, the number one factor in a child's education is the economic conditions in the home. You can take two students with different economic conditions in the home, and spend the same amount of money, time, and effort on both in the classroom; and statistically the one with the better economic home conditions will fair far better than the one without. Yet, isn't it ironic that most of the plans to improve education that we hear about involve taking more money out of the home, via taxes, making economic conditions worse in the home where it really counts? Does this make any sense?

It seems to me that if the government really wanted to make an educational impact they should be finding ways to get more money into the home, not less. But our educational shortfalls go much deeper than a failure to understand the greatest impact on a child's education.

In many school districts around the country, such as the Dallas Independent School District, teachers are forbidden to give lower than a 50% grade for any given grading period. The following is a recent press release that I received about how local citizens are trying to address this policy within the school district.

"Currently, district policy requires that the lowest grade a teacher may assign a student for any grading period is 50. Teachers tell us that this practice needs to change. In this new age of rigor, responsibility and accountability, teachers contend that grading policies must change to reflect these higher expectations. Your policy requires that grades be arbitrarily inflated. A student who submits not one assignment for the entire six weeks grading period, is still guaranteed a final grade of 50. To assign actual grades earned by students, instead of grades of not less than 50%, is a vital part of raising the achievement bar. An education is not something a child is given. An education is something the child must work for and earn. Before the board today is a policy proposal by EIA, local. If adopted, this policy continues the practice of assigning student grades not earned. What are we asking the board to do? Change your policy. Hold students accountable for their grades. Raise the bar. Increase student rigor. Allow teachers to assign students the grades they legitimately earned. Stop supporting grade inflation. Administrators claim that they inflate grades because if a student falls too far behind, then the student won't be able to catch up, no matter what they do."

In other words, the natural consequences are too great, so we have changed the rules.

While it may be true that certain children do fall behind and have a hard time making up the grades the rest of the year, lying to the students about the grades they receive is doing more harm than good. That's right, I said lying! Any school district that seeks to award any grade other than the grade that was earned by the student is dishonest in their actions, and is teaching the student that deceit is entirely acceptable. Do we really live in a world where it is acceptable to just change a score when we do not like it? Does anyone think that these children do not know what is going on, and that they do not figure out at an early age that the teachers and administrators are not going to hold them truly accountable?

If administrators are worried about the ill effects of poor grades, then they need to create a system to help kids catch up, and to keep them from falling behind in the first place. Instead, they have created a system that denies the truth as if it will just go away somehow. How can grades have any value if they are simply changed to protect the child from itself? How can we expect these children to be ready for employment in the real world if we are not honest with them in their youth?

The administrators of these school districts claim that they will not give a grade below a 50 because it "hurts the child", but I do not believe that they are being completely honest with us. I would suggest that our federal government and state governments have forced their hand with legislation like the "No Child Left Behind Act." This act has placed unreasonable expectations on districts around the nation. School districts are now changing their grading methods to make sure that their schools test scores remain in compliance, so that they do not miss out on much needed funding from the government. Once again, the feds stuck their nose into the problem and instead of helping; they guaranteed that the focus would be on everything but the legitimate success of our children.

Instead of focusing our efforts in the wrong places, we should be teaching our children that failure happens, and that it is a very important part of life. Failure helps us know when and where we need to improve.

Instead, we are taking away the ability to truly succeed by taking away the ability to fail. This is where we get back to the idea of the value of consequences, as described in one of the next chapters. Failure is there for a reason. The function of failure is to let you know that you have work to do and that the status quo simply will not be accepted. If we take away failure, then where is the measure of one's success? Truly, we cannot have success without the potential for failure, and there are no words that can convince a child or anyone else differently in the face of failure. Everyone must be able to fail in order to succeed.

Not only should we recognize failure, but we should embrace it as a sign that there is a concern and much work to be done. We need to teach our children that the potential for failure exists in everything they do, and that failure has clear consequences that will affect their entire lives. The true path to adulthood is learning to use our failures as a springboard to future success. Taking away that failure, or pretending it is not there, simply takes away any reason to try.

When I was in middle school, the students all knew the one boy who had been held back a year because he had failed the fourth grade. None of us wanted to be like him. This fear of failure motivated me to try harder and ensure that I was not held back. However, this fear no longer exists today because we do not acknowledge failure any longer. Our children know that no matter how poor their performance is they will be shuffled on to the next grade like everyone else. Then in the next grade, we have teachers that are supposed to be teaching the next level of education, but they cannot because children were passed on to them when they should have been held back. Additionally, teachers are facing more and more accountability today for passing rates, so they are then forced to move the kids on through, or face possible termination.

In other words, the failure to acknowledge failure has done nothing but guarantee failure.

The only people that should be involved in what our children learn is the parents, who vote for a school board, a school board who supervises a principal, and a principal who supervises the teachers. It should never be more complicated than that. The parents will hold the school board accountable, which will then work its way down the ladder to the teachers. It should be the principals' job to determine if a teacher is performing well, not the President of the United States. Through one-on-one interaction and feedback, only the principal can truly know what is happening in the classroom. It is his/her job to ensure proper instruction with the aid of the parents.

As far as accountability for what the student learns, national testing and even state testing has created an environment that ensures that proper instruction cannot happen. This testing needs to be thrown out, and we need to return to the way it used to be. In order to pass a class the student would have to perform to a certain expectation in several areas that would include testing, homework, class work, and participation. Each one of these areas would represent a certain percentage of their grade. The combined sum would have to be at least a certain percentage in order for them to progress to the next class or grade level. I am quite confident that this is how our universities of today continue to teach, but for some reason this type of system has been abandoned, in many, if not most districts across the country.

The truth is that most of what these students learn in their K-12 education will not be retained anyway. This is just a fact of life. Therefore, we can either teach them to answer questions on a test that they will not remember in the future, or we can teach them how to learn, and how to gain knowledge on their own throughout their lives. Instead of teaching them what to think, we should be teaching them how to think. Once a student has passed their final exam in a particular class subject, and has met the other requirements of the class, they should not have to return to that subject matter in the form of a test that comes at the end of their high school education -- or at the end of each year.

Here in California, we have students that are on the honor roll but are unable to pass the final state required test and are therefore denied a high school diploma. What nonsense! I do not believe that a high school diploma should be nothing more than a passing grade on a final test. Instead, it should show that this student worked diligently for four years and demonstrated a good working knowledge of the required material. No student should have to retain all of that instruction for some looming exam that determines their fate. The creator of this idea needs to take this test and we will see how well they do.

We have allowed our education system to become about dates, facts, and figures, when in truth; it should be about learning discipline, and the opening of the mind to bigger and better things. It should be about training people how to access information and process it for greater understanding. We have truly lost our way.

I am continually amazed at the things students are allowed to do in schools today without facing major discipline. Instead of discipline, these students face something called in-school suspension. What in the heck is in school suspension? You are still in school, so what is the point? Turns out that our schools do not want to send children home because they will lose precious federal dollars that we've been talking about -- as well as state funds -- that are based upon attendance numbers. So we are actually keeping kids in school that should not be there. These kids should be sent home to their parents until they shape up. I can promise you that once they become the problem of the parent, things will change! A free education should be available to all kids that are willing to follow the rules. The rest of them need to be sent home to Mom and Dad until they get the idea.

Our kids have figured out that they will not be facing any serious consequences for their actions, or lack of effort, so they continue to move in the wrong direction. Send them home and let's dedicate our time, tax dollars, and effort to those children who wish to be there. We may be surprised to find that once accountability is restored to the system that problem children rise to these higher standards.

One of the reasons that these schools are so reluctant to send their children home to Mom and Dad is because the parents come rushing back to school with an attorney complaining about the unfair treatment their son or daughter received. I believe that teachers are limited in the creative measures they can use in the classroom due to a fear of repercussions. Either legal or administrative. One of the most important things parents need to consider is that no teacher ever got into the field of education for the fame and fortune it brings, because it does not. Teachers teach because they care. We should trust what they are doing in the classroom until proven otherwise.

A good teacher should be like an extended family member. And as a member of the family, they should be able to hold these children accountable for their actions. Teachers spend a significant amount of time with our children and in an environment where they are free from the natural restraint they exhibit when in the company of their parents. Our teachers have the ability to see potential character traits of all kinds, and to acknowledge the good traits and curb the bad ones before they become habitual. They are a big part of what kind of person our kids will become once they grow up. We should appreciate their help and give them more credit.

While we are on the subject, once again I want to say that we should stop trying to protect our children from failure! Remember, every time you come to their rescue, you are denying them an opportunity to learn the realities of life. The sooner they learn these lessons, the better. If you truly love them, you will let them feel the pain of failure once in a while. Afterward, teach them how to get over it properly. Otherwise, we are going to raise a generation of pansies, who cannot operate effectively in the real world.

Educate and inform the whole mass of the people... They are the only sure reliance for the preservation of our liberty.

~ *Thomas Jefferson*

Now let's get back to the idea that local communities should be in charge of the education of their children, not the federal government. If we can ever return to this type of system, we will begin to see innovation in education once again. What I mean is that one school district will try something new, and it will result in great success, so other districts will want to employ the same principles. This type of innovation is stomped out today by the federal government and their insistence on making everyone play the same tune. State governments do it as well. But once again, by way of the best intentions, we are guaranteeing that there will be limited change. The larger the program is, the harder it is to control, and the less innovation there will be. We must learn this truth as we hear those who wish to lead our country clamor forever more government control and interference in education.

A Different Way to Look at Education

My final thought about education comes from my own unorthodox schooling, and from the experiences of my life to date. I believe that we might be making a mistake in grouping children together in school merely by age. A common age does not indicate a common learning ability. Having spent a good portion of my life training and observing others, it has become very clear to me that our minds do not all process data in the same way. I would be interested in seeing if there was some fair and non-discriminatory way, to see if we could separate them by learning ability instead of by age.

The obvious concern here is that some kids could get left behind by a system that, for whatever reason, allowed something other than learning ability determine what course study they received. This is another one of those ideas that possess an interesting intellectual question.

I began thinking about this concept in my mid-twenties when I was given the job of learning a new database system for the company I worked for. This was a 'train-the-trainer' situation and once I learned the system, I had the task of training all of the department heads in my company to use the new system. After mastering the system myself, I held several group-training sessions for all the managers and then I set a one day appointment with each one, during which time I would train them on the module of the program that was specific to their department. However, I set a two day appointment with one of the managers, knowing that a single day of training would simply not be enough for him. It wasn't that this manager was not as smart as the others; instead, I knew that he processed information very differently and would therefore, require more training time. You see, his mind had to understand every little aspect of the system. He needed to understand the individual "hows" and the "whys" of the entire system before he could map the bigger picture in his head. Unless he understood step A completely, he could never move on to steps B, or C. Once he learned the system, he knew it better than almost everyone else, and could train just about anyone on how to use it. He just learned differently than the others. I don't believe that this was an issue of intelligence; instead, it was something more complicated. Since then I have thought of it more as an individualized learning curve.

In my own case, I capture information and learn things at a very rapid pace. Because of this, I get bored very quickly in training meetings, and in school, because I don't want to wait around for people to catch up. Also, if a subject interests me, I become almost obsessive in learning every detail I can find on it and have a near 100% retention of even the most obscure details. Again, I do not look at this as being smarter than those around me are. I just capture things faster. I can't help but wonder how many students there are in our school systems across the country that are bored out of their minds, and possibly acting out as a result like I did as a teenager.

I also wonder how many of these children are being medicated instead of being challenged. This thought concerns me more than you can imagine because of the long-term implications it possess for future generations.

Wouldn't it make more sense to assess learning curves at an early age and then make an attempt to group children together based upon how they learn? We could then let them progress through the material at whatever pace would be comfortable for them. I think we might find a higher number of kids that are able to get through a 12-year program in much less time than we do today. I also believe that we would have fewer problems with children acting out, because they would be engaged and challenged instead of bored and impatient. We might also discover possible anti-social effects by not learning with kids of their age or any number of unintended consequences. But it is an interesting concept, nonetheless.

In my own case, in high school I was what could best be described as a "challenging" student. I was bored by the subject matter, stifled by the traditional expectations, unwilling to accept the status quo, rebellious simply for the sake of rebellion and just smart enough to be a real pain in the neck to those in authority. I challenged everything and everyone. I also did not have a clue about why I was doing any of this at the time. I just did not like school. Instead, I went out and educated myself because I felt that at least then I could control the pace and the subject matter. And, had it not been for one teacher, I might have just walked away from school and never looked back. But this teacher challenged me in the right ways at just the right times to keep me from making a huge mistake in my life. I am proud today to have him as my friend.

As an adult, it seems like I have spent most of my time in one classroom or another, either as a student or an instructor. Today I enjoy learning about all kinds of subjects and sharing them with others. And, I am told that I am very good at teaching. I believe this is because I share information in the way I would like to receive it, and I try to have fun doing so. It also helps that I am not shy about telling people what I think. But, had I given up on education, I would have missed some of the most personally fulfilling times of my life.

Regardless of how we go about educating our children, we must acknowledge that a basic cost of our freedom is that, as much as we may think otherwise, the federal government cannot solve the problems that we face -- and in most cases will simply make them worse.

Summary

One of the most basic costs of our freedom is the recognition that, although we would like to think that a bigger government could solve all problems, in reality, government always fails in trying to do so. But more important than that is the fact that this is simply not their role. The proper role of government is to protect all people equally, not to take away protections from some in order to advance the situation of others. Not to try to tell us how much of our own money we can keep, how we should raise our children, how think, how to feel, what we can do with our bodies or even who we can marry. The more government gets involved in our lives, the fewer freedoms we the people will enjoy and the more money it spends. Remember that the government should do its best to guarantee equality of opportunity, but it can never, and should never try to create equality of outcome. Doing so would only make us equally poor, or equally mediocre. A free society simply must resist the temptation of looking to the government for solutions to most of our problems.

.

3.
THE PRICE OF PARTISANSHIP

"Every government degenerates when trusted to the rulers of the people alone. The people themselves, therefore, are its only safe depositories."

~ Thomas Jefferson, Notes on the State of Virginia, Query 14, 1781

The frustration of the people of the United States with their government seems to be at an all-time high. More and more people come to me and express their opinion that our representatives are out of control and that there is simply no hope in ever solving the problem. "The politicians only cater to those who have the money," these concerned citizens also say that the voices of the people will never be heard. Many folks have even expressed the idea that the only way to get control over our government again is to grab our torches and pitchforks and march on the Capital. I always respond to them with one question, "and then what?" The typical response I get to this question is that these revolutionaries would return to the type of government that was intended by the founding fathers. Then I ask "How do we do that."

No one ever has an answer for that question.

To those of you, who feel this desperation; believe me when I tell you I feel your pain. But I would suggest to you that the majority of United States citizens do not quite understand the power that the Constitution gives them. The founding fathers knew that politicians would be easily corrupted by money and power, which is precisely why they designed a system of checks and balances.

Just about everyone is familiar with the separation of powers to ensure that no one government agency or official could gain power over all the others. Unfortunately, most people do not realize that the founders established a much greater check and balance against corruption when they created a representative government. It was known by our founders that the power of government would almost certainly corrupt individual politicians. They believed that the people, given the responsibility and authority, would vote out any corrupt or ineffective politicians; instead of voting them in again, year after year. Unfortunately, somewhere along the way, the people have forgotten about this responsibility and their duty to cleanse the government of corruption. The reality is the fact that the people seem to have willingly turned this power over to the political parties, expecting them to carry the water for everyone else. The problem with this idea is that it asks the politicians to police themselves. You don't need to be Albert Einstein to understand how unrealistic of a concept this is. It virtually eliminates the all-important checks and balances of representation installed by our founders and leaves the citizens open to all sorts of abuse of power. If you don't believe that this is the case let me ask you a few questions:

1) If an elected official breaks his/her campaign promises to the people is it possible that he/she can still be re-elected?

2) If an elected official goes against his/her party lines, can they be re-elected?

3) If an elected official goes against the special interest groups or corporations that helped them get elected can he/she be re-elected?

Sadly, the answer to question one is "very likely" and the answer to questions two and three is "not very likely." So whom do you think your elected officials represent; you, or their parties, special interest groups, and campaign contributors?

The truth is that our representatives do not fear our will as much as they do the will of their party and big money special interest groups. The primary reason for this is that they have managed to divide the majority of us into two tidy little groups that they know, on election day will vote for all Democrats or for all Republicans. This then frees the parties up to be able to sell those guaranteed voting blocks to the highest special interest "bidder". Asking political parties to police their own politicians is like asking an addict to keep an eye on the pharmacy. It simply is not logical and obviously does not work.

Our very first president, George Washington, saw the apathy of the people coming and went so far as to tell people what would happen if they were not "ever vigilant" in fighting for and protecting their rights. He also warned about what would come if they relied too heavily on a political party system. In his farewell address to the nation, he warned the people not to get involved in, or to affiliate themselves with political parties. He correctly believed that they would be the downfall of this country. Almost as if he could see into the future, President Washington told the people exactly what the result would be if we all joined parties and became divided. His words that day were nothing short of prophetic. Their veracity is proven every single day in this country of partisan politics.

The following are some of his words and how I believe they apply to our time. Keep in mind that the language and grammar of that day was very different, and that the following quotes are directly from his written notes. Sometimes the language is a little difficult to understand, and you may have to read each quote several times for it to really sink in. To help clarify, I have tried to do my best in describing what I believe he meant.

As you read our first President's words, please consider the fact that Gen. Washington did not wish to be the President of the United States. He accepted the role to serve the nation that he fought for, and so dearly loved. In fact, most of the great leaders throughout history, like Washington, never sought to hold any historic role, but only responded when called by history and circumstance. Many, such as Washington, felt duty bound and assumed the responsibility only after much persuasion was wielded by their contemporaries. After his first term, the people begged Mr. Washington to stay, and he reluctantly accepted. He finally refused a third term, which was basically his for the taking. My point is that this was a man who, by most accounts, put his country over everything else, including any personal desire for wealth or political power. So as you read the words from his farewell address, please consider the intent of his heart, and the quality of his character.

First, George Washington believed that we should never allow ourselves to be divided by party platforms. He continually expressed the need for unity over division when he said the following;

"The Unity of Government which constitutes you one people is also now dear to you. It is justly so; for it is a main Pillar in the Edifice of your real independence, the support of your tranquility at home; your peace abroad; of your safety; of your prosperity; of that very Liberty which you so highly prize."

More plainly said; "united we stand, divided we fall." Can you say that we have any sort of real "Unity" of government today? If not, why? To me, the answer is very clear; our two party system. Political parties, by their very nature, are designed to divide a people that should be united in our commonality as citizens, and a two party system creates nothing more than a tug-o-war for political power giving one side reason to work against the other instead of for the country as a whole. How could unity come out of a situation like this?

In this next statement, George Washington directly linked our independence, tranquility, peace, safety, prosperity, and liberty to "unity." Mr. Washington then went on to warn the people against political divisions based upon geographical conditions as we saw with the Civil War, or even as we see now as we draw hard lines based upon any number of items such as economics, political beliefs, party affiliation (red and blue states) or even race:

"In contemplating the causes which may disturb our Union, it occurs as matter of serious concern, that any ground should have been furnished for characterizing parties by Geographical discriminations-- Northern and Southern--Atlantic and Western; whence designing men may endeavour to excite a belief that there is a real difference of local interests and views ."

"One of the expedients of Party to acquire influence, within particular districts, is to misrepresent the opinions & aims of other Districts. You cannot shield yourselves too much against the jealousies & heart burnings, which spring from these misrepresentations. They tend to render Alien to each other that who ought to be bound together by fraternal Affection."

"To the efficacy and permanency of Your Union, a Government for the whole is indispensable. No Alliances however strict between the parts can be an adequate substitute. They must inevitably experience the infractions & interruptions which all Alliances in all times have experienced."

Do we ever see one party misrepresenting the opinions and aims of the other party today? Is it not true that your party affiliation creates "jealousies and heart burnings" because of these representations? Have our party affiliations caused us to look at those in other parties as "aliens" when we ought to be bound together as Americans? Do the political parties ever have problems trusting each other or working together these days? As far as I can tell, these things only happen on days of the week that end in the letter "Y". Our first president suggested that we should let no affiliation allow us to be divided as Americans and that is pretty good advice.

As we watch our representatives battle it out on Capitol Hill, the question of whether or not a particular initiative is good for the country simply never comes up. Instead, the support of one party or another, for any program, is determined by how the program's passage will help that party gain advantage over the other. What is best for America and its citizens has become irrelevant. The actual will of the people is hardly ever taken into consideration and is most certainly never a factor in how the party leadership thinks or acts.

"They (parties) serve to Organize faction, to give it an artificial and extraordinary force--to put in the place of the delegated will of the Nation, the will of a party; often a small but artful and enterprizing minority of the Community; and, according to the alternate triumphs of different parties, to make the public Administration the Mirror of the ill concerted and incongruous projects of faction, rather than the Organ of consistent and wholesome plans digested by common councils and modified by mutual interests. However combinations or Associations of the above description may now & then answer popular ends, they are likely, in the course of time and things, to become potent engines, by which cunning, ambitious and unprincipled men will be enabled to subvert the Power of the People, & to usurp for themselves the reins of Government; destroying afterwards the very engines which have lifted them to unjust dominion."

Do we not see this everywhere today; the delegated will of the people being usurped by the will of one party or the other? Do we also see that it is the radicals of these parties, who are a minority, are actually controlling the majority? Do we see parties causing or hoping that a program under the control of the opposing party will fail in order to make that party look bad? Is this not exactly what we saw with the war in Iraq or the debt ceiling talks or the Universal Healthcare legislation? This is really a very simple concept; when two teams enter the playing field everyone understands that one will win and the other will lose. More and more, we see the party out of power hoping for a poor economy, or a major policy failure so that there can be a shift in power.

How is this good for the country? This is not a game to be won or lost; it is about doing what is right for America. Shouldn't we be rooting for the success of our elected representatives regardless of who is in power? Our first president then took a moment to warn us about allowing changes to our basic principles of government:

"Towards the preservation of your Government and the permanency of your present happy state, it is requisite, not only that you steadily discountenance irregular oppositions to its acknowledged authority, but also that you resist with care the spirit of innovation upon its principles however specious the pretexts."

As if he was viewing our day, George Washington then went on to discuss the problems that can arise from any party affiliation, geographic or otherwise:

"I have already intimated to you the danger of Parties in the State, with particular reference to the founding of them on Geographical discriminations. Let me now take a more comprehensive view, & warn you in the most solemn manner against the baneful effects of the Spirit of Party, generally. This Spirit, unfortunately, is inseparable from our nature, having its root in the strongest passions of the human Mind. It exists under different shapes in all Governments, more or less stifled, controuled, or repressed; but in those of the popular form it is seen in its greatest rankness and is truly their worst enemy. The alternate domination of one faction over another, sharpened by the spirit of revenge natural to party dissention , which in different ages & countries has perpetrated the most horrid enormities, is itself a frightful despotism. But this leads at length to a more formal and permanent despotism. The disorders & miseries, which result, gradually incline the minds of men to seek security & repose in the absolute power of an Individual: and sooner or later the chief of some prevailing faction more able or more fortunate than his competitors, turns this disposition to the purposes of his own elevation, on the ruins of Public Liberty."

"...the common & continual mischiefs of the spirit of Party are sufficient to make it the interest and the duty of a wise People to discourage and restrain it."

See if any of the following warnings from President Washington, all from his farewell address, have come true in our day regarding political parties;

"It serves always to distract the Public Councils and enfeeble the Public Administration."

"Kindles the animosity of one part against another,"

"Foments occasionally riot & insurrection."

"It opens the door to foreign influence & corruption, which find a facilitated access to the government itself through the channels of party passions. Thus the policy and the will of one country are subjected to the policy and will of another."

Our first President also spoke to those who believe that parties do serve a valuable purpose in a free society:

"There is an opinion that parties in free countries are useful checks upon the Administration of the Government and serve to keep alive the spirit of Liberty. This within certain limits is probably true--and in Governments of a Monarchical cast Patriotism may look with endulgence, if not with favour, upon the spirit of party. But in those of the popular character, in Governments purely elective, it is a spirit not to be encouraged."

"From their natural tendency, it is certain there will always be enough of that spirit for every salutary purpose. And there being constant danger of excess, the effort ought to be, by force of public opinion, to mitigate & assuage it. A fire not to be quenched; it demands a uniform vigilance to prevent its bursting into a flame, lest instead of warming it should consume."

While most political organizations are founded for proper reasons, eventually they lose sight of their original purpose, and replace that purpose with more base survival and power motives. The survival and status of the party becomes more important than responding to the needs and the will of the people. Each party survives and gains power largely by attacking the other party or opposing groups, and generally creating division among the people. I would submit to you that all of George Washington's warnings about party affiliation have come true in our time. We are a people divided! We have allowed the parties to usurp our power and responsibility! We have fallen asleep at the wheel! The ironic thing is that the parties have convinced us that this is the way it's supposed to be. But just so you know, political parties are not part of the Constitution, and the so-called political aisle that divides Congress and the nation is a creation of those who seek personal power over the good of this nation. If they are allowed to continue to do so, it will only be because the people have shirked their responsibility, and have failed to heed the warnings of our first president.

Fortunately, there is a solution which has very little to do with torches and pitchforks. This solution has everything to do with fulfilling the responsibility bestowed upon us by the founders of this nation. This is where the cost part of the freedom equation comes in. We must become Americans again. No longer can we be a people divided. We must no longer enter the election booth and look for all the "R's" or all the "D's." We must stop letting ourselves be defined by political affiliations. The simple fact is that we increase the power of the people by decreasing the power of the parties. If the American people were to jump off the mainstream party membership rolls en-mass, our representatives would be forced to come to us once again. Yes, we do need a revolution; a revolution of representation, and revulsion of party affiliation.

Only then can we expect to return this government to the state that it was intended to be.

In the end, if this great experiment in government fails, it will not be because of war or economic failure. Instead, it will be because the people who were left in charge (its citizens) shirked their responsibility and proved that the founders of this nation were wrong to entrust its citizens with this sacred responsibility. Perhaps an aristocracy or dictatorship was the way to go after all. I can only pray that the founders were right to entrust us with this duty, and that we will all wake up and fulfill our responsibility before it is too late.

Now this does not mean that we will not still have our differences, of course people who live in the northwest part of the country will naturally have a few different priorities than those who live southwest deserts. That's obvious. But the key is not to let our party affiliations define those differences. Why can't a person be "Pro Life" and "Pro Environment" at the same time? How about "Fiscally Conservative" and "Pro Universal Health-Care"? I have never understood how or why we would allow our partisan affiliation to shape what we think about anything. When we are confronted with an important issue, we should not be letting party affiliation tell us how we should view the issue. Nor should we be worried about whether the cause of the problem, or the solution, will make our party look better or worse. We should be seeing things for how they really are, and how they really affect Americans, not looking at issues for how they can be packaged to fit in with our partisan affiliations.

Democrats claim to believe in civil liberties and that the government should not tell you how to live and what to do. But Democrats are the first to take away your money and tell you how you can spend it. Doesn't anyone see a contradiction there? The Republicans believe that the government should be as small as possible, yet they seem to love getting involved in legislating morality, and lately, the implementation of government agencies and spending which requires bigger government. Our parties are filled with contradictions, yet because there are only two of them, we cling to one or the other like a toddler to his favorite blanket. Sadly, we can only blame ourselves for this, and it's up to us to stop it.

One of the best examples that I can think of as to how the two party systems has clouded our judgment came in the days after the election of President Obama. I cannot tell you how many people I spoke with who made the comment that they were hoping that President Obama would fall flat on his face. They were hoping for his failure so that a Republican could be put back in the White House. Honestly, these comments shocked me because they clearly showed a desire for party success over the betterment of the country as a whole. Can it really be considered patriotic to wish for the country's failure so that your political party can regain power? Wouldn't it be more appropriate to hope that regardless of what party the president is a member of, that he is able to lead this country to better things? I barely supported any of Geo. W. Bush' policies, but I never wished for him to fail or do something that would cause major damage to the country. I can say the same thing about Pres. Obama. I do not care about party affiliation. Once they are in office they become "My" elected representative. When they succeed, we all succeed. If they fail, we all fail.

I have one final thought on this subject that I would like you to consider; "Does it make sense in a country of over 300 million people that we are truly represented by a system that limits itself to only 2 parties?" This is not logical. I cannot believe that this country could agree on two types of ice cream much less two types of political ideologies. If we are going to stick with political partisanship than we need more than just "Liberal" and "Conservative" to choose from to adequately cover the various viewpoints and differing opinions of the population today. We need 10 or 20, maybe even more, legitimately accepted parties to really represent the ideological cross-section we have in this country today. If we had just a couple more parties holding seats in congress then, by definition, any legislation that is passed would have required multi-partisan support. Multi-partisanship is one of the best ways to ensure that those in government do not forget about the people who put them there. It ensures a wider range of opinions are included in the decision making process and it can almost guarantee that one party will never have enough power to block the will of the people simply by gaining a majority of seats in congress. How could that be a bad thing?

Term Limits

Occasionally we hear cries for mandatory term limits for congress and other elected officials. But I would suggest to you that term limits are a lazy man's form of representative government. If an elected official is doing a poor job, then the people need to get rid of him/her. Conversely, if a representative is doing a fantastic job, then why shouldn't they be able to stay in office and continue to serve the will and needs of the people? We should not be looking for laws to do the job that our founders asked us to do. We need to participate in the process. That is the only way we can be sure it is working.

Summary

One of the primary costs of freedom in our society is that we must be vigilant in holding our representatives accountable. Asking political parties to do so has put us in a place where we have some of the lowest approval ratings for federal elected officials in our country's history. Party leaders have created the "politics of division" mentality that is prohibiting our representatives from doing their jobs and are allowing a large portion of the population not to have to think very hard about their party's motives. That even under the best circumstances, most parties will eventually shift focus from the work of governing to its own preservation and advancement. That a two party system is not the solution; it is a big part of the problem. Until we are willing to pay the cost and demand representation, we simply deserve what we get. We have to find a way to get the political parties to listen to our will, or we must do away with these parties altogether. And if we are unwilling to do that, we need to change our system so that it provides a greater variety of parties to choose from. Additionally, if the people feel like they are not adequately represented then it is the fault of the people, as well as the representatives. And finally, are we willing to pay the cost of time and effort to ensure we have a truly representative government?

4.
THE COST OF CONFLICT

"[I]t is a common observation here that our cause is the cause of all mankind, and that we are fighting for their liberty in defending our own."

~ *Benjamin Franklin, letter to Samuel Cooper, May 1, 1777*

————————————————— ✦ ✦ ✦ —————————————————

This is probably the most easily understood cost of our freedom; considering that we have lost lives on the battlefield in the name of gaining those freedoms. In fact, every right and freedom we enjoy today came from horrendous battles where thousands gave their lives for the cause of freedom. Yet, somewhere along the way, many Americans decided that the cost of our freedom is the wars of the past, and that this cost has been paid in full. This will never be true because of one simple reason; there are plenty of 'bad guys' in the world. We have to remember that there will always be those who seek to gain by stepping over other people. It's human nature! No matter how benevolent we are as a nation, or as individuals, there will be those who seek to take away our freedoms, and our very lives, without provocation. We can never forget this fact. Our very freedom depends upon it.

The most basic cost of our freedom is that we must be prepared to give our lives to protect our freedoms.

As such, we must always make sure that we have the best technology, and the means to deploy forces, at any time. As much, I hate to admit, I simply cannot imagine a time when the United States will not need a standing military. Plus, with the introduction of weapons of mass destruction into the equation, we have to be even more vigilant and involved in international matters than ever before.

I am afraid that we have come to a new time and place in our society where many, if not most, believe that we can stick to our own business, and let the rest of the world go on its merry way -- and in doing so, we won't get hurt. We have been here before. This is a lesson learned from history. Several times in our past, a large number of Americans have held strong isolationist beliefs. It is easy to understand how that could happen. One could take comfort from the idea of "not getting involved" in foreign disputes. The problem is that this strategy has not had much, if any, success and as a result of increases in population, advances in communication, travel and information sharing technology the world is getting smaller by the day. As a result, we just do not have the luxury of sticking our heads in the sand any more. If someone can build a bomb in a foreign country one day and detonate that bomb here the next, then everybody needs to understand we are not going to just sit back and let it happen.

"If we desire to avoid insult, we must be able to repel it; if we desire to secure peace, one of the most powerful instruments of our rising prosperity, it must be known, that we are at all times ready for War."

~ George Washington

The biggest problem that I see for this country is how we use the power that this country commands. America is at a unique point in history. Since the fall of the former Soviet Union, right or wrong, the United States is considered the "last superpower". But, observing how our elected representatives have engaged the rest of the world since then, it seems as though America is having an identity crisis. Some days we act like a giant who does not understand his strength and walks around breaking things by accident. Some days we seem to be the shy kid in class who never wants to participate. At the turn of the last century, we became the spoiled, self-absorbed rich kid who does whatever makes him feel good and in the last couple of years, we have been the handicapped person that has problems getting anything done.

In the 1990's, President Clinton tried to be the moral leader of the world by engaging our troops in the conflicts of Somalia and the Balkans but failed to have the strength of character necessary to stay the course under public pressure. Then, President Bush did his best to "act" presidential in response to the attacks of Sept. 11, 2001 but, because it was an act, he ended up becoming what I think of as the "class bully" due to a fundamental lack of intellect and the belief that no one could challenge his agenda. Both made huge mistakes for very different reasons. Both ultimately hurt our nation and its international standing in very similar ways.

By not standing firm in Somalia and not reacting faster to the genocide in the Balkans, Clinton left the world with an image of a weak, self-absorbed nation that had no "compass" in regards to foreign relations. He left the international community uncertain of our commitment or desire to honor our treaty's and live up to our obligations as a global neighbor. Bush on the other hand, used fear and subterfuge to take advantage of the attacks of 9/11 to push an ultra-conservative agenda by misrepresenting facts, stifling dissent and leading us down a path that ended in war with Iraq.

President Bush did get one thing right. If the evidence to support Osama bin Laden was in fact responsible for the attacks of 9/11 is correct, then Bush's invasion of Afghanistan was right and proper. America was attacked and we had every right, and the responsibility, to fight back. Although, this situation had some highly unusual circumstances to take into consideration, Mr. Bush and his advisors handled the challenges we faced in the best manner available.

For the first time in history the United States were attacked not by another nation, but by what can best be described as a private guerrilla organization (al Qaeda) that existed independently within a country (Afghanistan) whose leadership (the Taliban) had not participated in the planning, or had foreknowledge, of the attacks on 9/11/2001. Although the Taliban was providing diplomatic protection to the leadership of the al Qaede there is no evidence that they actively participated. Our enemy, al Qaeda, had no address, no infrastructure to attack, no diplomatic corp., no military to meet on a battlefield and no borders to defend. They didn't even have a flag!

After a bumpy start, Bush correctly faced these challenges in the days immediately following 9/11. He addressed the nation and defined our intentions by stating that America would "...pursue those responsible and those who harbor those responsible...". America entered Afghanistan with the mission of "rooting out the evil-doer" and in doing so, we found allies in the Northern Alliance, a group engaged in an internal struggle for control of Afghanistan against the Taliban. Neither group was our intended target. Yet the Taliban chose to pick up arms and fight against us. I believe that if they had not, America would have simply sought out the leaders of al Qaeda and taken them into custody. I also believe we would not have found it necessary to engage in regime change that got us bogged down for a decade helping rebuild a nation.

If Bush had limited his aggression to just going after those who actually attacked us, it would be a much different world today. But, he did not. Instead, he saw this as a perfect opportunity to advance the cause of a group of his friends at the "Project for a New American Century". Bush pursued an agenda that, for many reasons, fit his worldview, political ideology and self-image. He chose to expand his "war on terror" and "go after those who would hurt America, wherever they may be". In effect, our president concluded that he and his friends alone could decide who the terrorists were and whether or not they might try to harm this country. This is not only unprecedented and dangerous; it goes against everything this country is supposed to stand for. If you were able to ask Bush today (and if he answered honestly), I am sure he would say it was probably the best chance he was going to get to push his agenda. This was his chance to invade Iraq.

It is a well-established fact that since taking office in Jan 2001 members of the administration had been looking at ways to invade Iraq. Bush's National Security team held several meetings with Iraq as the main topic starting in Jan 2001. His Secretary of Defense was updating operational assessments for Iraq as early as April 2001. Vice President Cheney was given authority to create an 'Energy Task Force' in March 2001 whose notes have not been released to this day. Although, eight pages were accidentally turned over by the State Department, under a freedom of information request. These documents contained maps of the Iraqi oil fields and notes written in the margins that indicated how those fields were to be divided up among the major oil companies to begin exploitation --- 6 months before 9/11. These actions and many others show the clear motive and established intent on the part of the administration to invade Iraq regardless of public opinion.

No other reasonable explanation could exist based on the facts that have come out over the years since. I have reached this conclusion not because of a difference in political ideology or a belief in some complicated conspiracy theory. Rather, I reached this conclusion because it is the simplest explanation that can account for all the actions, misinformation, leaks, lies, and ultimately the outcome achieved by his administration.

My position on the Bush administration is based on the fact that every step they took in regards to Iraqi planning, both before and after 9/11, were done under an unprecedented veil of secrecy. I was taught that in a Democracy, the only reason someone needs to take actions in secret is that the virtue of those actions will not stand up under the light of day. Additionally, the administration went to great lengths to link Saddam Hussein to the attacks of 9/11 and to establish a public belief that Saddam had, or was seeking, methods to attack the U.S. with WMD. Both of which can only be believed by making incredible leaps of faith and overlooking verified information to the contrary. Only someone, or some group, who is trying to hide ulterior motives would come up with this type of scenario to explain or justify their intended course of action.

It's that simple. They wanted to remove Saddam and get their hands on the second largest untapped oil reserves on the planet and came up with a cover story to convince the world that it was to protect us from the evil intentions of an unstable dictator.

And this drives me nuts because, the real shame, and possible crime, in President Bush's actions is that the U.S. already had legitimate cause and legal right to go after Saddam if they wanted to. There was no need to resort to the wholesale misrepresentation of facts and creating bogus justifications. Yet they chose to manipulate the public in our national moment of weakness following Sept. 11 because they thought it would be an easier "sell" than going after him for legitimate, although very technical, reasons.

To those of you who have questioned the validity of war against Saddam (as opposed to the reasons for), I must ask; at what point would you have approved of an intervention in Iraq? Apparently, the murder of hundreds of thousands of innocent lives is not quite enough to sway your opinion. How about the fact he repeatedly violated the terms ending the 1991 Gulf War? Maybe knowing that Saddam illegally used the money, Iraq received during the 'Oil for Food" program to buy weapons might have gotten you to re-assess your thinking. Or would you have joined the battle cry if Iraq were sending millions to the gas chamber as Hitler did? If not, then you have failed to learn from history, and you seem willing to repeat it; even if it means World War III.

The reality is that World War II could have been stopped long before it started, if we would only have reacted to the warning signs. However, instead of dealing with Hitler when these warning signs became visible, the anti-war groups of the world sought to reason with the unreasonable; resulting in the most costly war in world history. Unfortunately, many have either forgotten history or failed to learn about WWII in the first place -- so I feel that this is an appropriate time to revisit the events of the past.

The right of a nation to kill a tyrant in case of necessity can no more is doubted than to hang a robber, or kill a flea.

~ *John Adams*

A Short History Lesson

The first opportunity that the world had to stop World War II came in 1933 when Hitler began re-arming Germany. This was a direct violation of the Treaty of Versailles. Instead of forcing Germany to uphold its end of the treaty, Great Britain and France put their heads in the sand, convincing themselves that Hitler was not a threat.

In 1936, Hitler fired another warning shot across the bow of Great Britain and France when he invaded the Rhineland that separated Germany and France. This act was once again in violation of the Treaty of Versailles and the Locarno Pact between France and Germany. Interestingly, the French had more than sufficient military in the Rhineland to resist Germany, but France did not want to act without Britain's support. So France just handed the Rhineland over to Hitler without resistance. Hitler appeased the world by promising that the Rhineland was Germany's last territorial demand in Europe and that Germany will never break the peace. In allowing Hitler to move forward without reprisal the world had missed its second opportunity to stop WWII.

Adolph Hitler came to believe that the world would not, or could not stop his actions, because up until that time France and Great Britain had refused to enforce their threats -- even though the treaty gave them absolute authority to do so. In 1938, without fear of reprisal, Hitler seized Vienna and annexed Austria. Once again, the world sat idly by, allowing Germany's actions to go unchecked. The world had now been given three opportunities to avoid a world war. Yet, the appeasers and the "America Foresters" as they were called, continued to prevail, and no action was taken to stop the evil dictator.

Hitler's next move was to demand the Sudetenland from Czechoslovakia, saying that it would be his last territorial demand in Europe. The Czechs wanted no part of Hitler's demands so they armed for war in order to defend their land. Here again, instead of seeing the warning signs, Great Britain and France went the route of appeasement. British Prime Minister Chamberlain went to Germany and struck a deal with Adolph. In exchange for a signed agreement with Hitler that Germany would settle all of its future differences with Europe peacefully, Prime Minister Chamberlain surrendered the Sudetenland. The Prime Minister returned to Great Britain waiving the signed document from Hitler stating that it would grant peace in their time. Instead of seeing the fourth warning sign of WWII, the world closed its eyes and put its fingers in its ears, proclaiming that all was well, because Hitler had signed a piece of paper.

Six months after Hitler signed this document he drove into Prague and assumed complete control of Czechoslovakia. Once again, no country stood up to him.

Why wouldn't he think that he could conquer the entire planet? Wouldn't you? Finally, after all their treaties and warnings, Great Britain and France began to see the writing on the wall. Both countries gave notice that if Germany invaded Poland they would declare war. Unfortunately, by this time it was too late. Hitler's war machine was too powerful to be stopped without U.S. Intervention.

On September 1, 1939, fifty-six German divisions crashed into Poland. Britain and France finally declared war on Germany. In the United States President FDR began to warn the people that the "war is a contagion" and that the U.S. must act. However, the appeasers and isolationists could not see how Germany's actions could reach American soil. The United States failed again to act at that time.

In 1940, Hitler rolled over Denmark, Norway, Luxembourg, Belgium, the Netherlands, and then marched into Paris. The United

States still failed to act and France fell to the Germans. Meanwhile, millions of Jews were being led to their deaths. Again, the United States failed to act. Adolph Hitler then began his assault on Great Britain. The new Prime Minister, Winston Churchill pleaded with the United States to give him the tools so he could finish the job.

Finally, in 1941, after countless warning signs, and the loss of millions of lives, FDR decided to start sending aide to Great Britain. He stated that the United States must become "the arsenal of democracy." In response to FDR's request, congress passed the Lend-Lease Act, which finally allowed the United States to abandon its neutrality status. American supply ships began crossing the sea to help fight the battle against Germany.

Many people are under the mistaken belief that the Pearl Harbor attack is what forced the United States into World War II, when in fact; America was already involved in a naval war with Germany before December 7, 1941. The United States supply line to Great Britain was helping to turn the tide against Germany, so Hitler sent his fleet of U-boats to take out American supply ships. Even if the Pearl Harbor attack never happened, the United States was destined for a declaration of war against Germany.

Fortunately, the United States did get involved, and eventually Germany, Japan, and Italy were put down; but at a cost of how many lives? How different would world history be if France and Great Britain had responded to the first sign of trouble from Hitler, instead of trying to appease his insanity? The lack of action on the part of these countries encouraged Hitler and made him believe that no nation could stand against him. Moreover, the United States neutrality policy ensured that America was not a threat to his designs. The thing that makes this failure to act so infuriating is that the Treaty of Versailles gave them the authority to put down Hitler at every turn. In my mind, this is one of the greatest lessons to be learned from World War II, that given the chance, we cannot fail to enforce treaties against those who show clear signs of aggression towards other countries.

In 1991, history began to repeat itself as a dictator named Saddam Hussein tried to capture the world's oil supply by rolling over his neighboring country of Kuwait. Like Hitler, Saddam believed that the world would not stop him. Fortunately, Saddam was wrong, and the

United Nations did not take the road of appeasement. Saddam was sent back to Baghdad with his tail between his legs.

Unfortunately, we did not remove Saddam from power when we had the chance. In retrospect, this was probably a huge mistake. Instead, we opted for a cease-fire agreement with the hope that Saddam had learned his lesson -- and that he would follow the terms to which he put his signature.

Once the smoke from the Gulf War had cleared and President Clinton entered the White House, Saddam Hussein slowly began to violate his treaty with the United Nations. Every time he did so, instead of enforcing the treaty, Bill Clinton and the United Nations would move the line backwards; much like France and Great Britain did when they refused to enforce the Treaty of Versailles. Just like Hitler, Saddam Hussein was encouraged by this lack of action and his efforts became more brazen. He also saw the weakness shown in Somalia and the Balkans as an indication of our desire to avoid conflict at any cost. Soon, he was re-arming his country using money from the "Oil for Food" program, which was supposed to be feeding his people. Again, the United Nations and President Clinton did nothing. By the time George Bush became the President of the United States, Saddam Hussein had managed to go against every tenant of his treaty with the United Nations– and Saddam had succeeded in getting the weapon inspectors removed from Iraq.

On September 11, 2001, a group of nineteen terrorist hijacked several jetliners and crashed them into the World Trade Center, the Pentagon, and a Pennsylvania field; causing more death and devastation than the attack on Pearl Harbor. At this time, President Bush came to the unrealistic decision that the only way to fight terrorism is to take the war to, not only the terrorists who were responsible, but also anyone else he saw as a threat. The era of appeasement in the 1990's had done nothing but strengthen his resolve and put our safety at further risk.

Bush's first target of the war on terrorism was Afghanistan, where the Taliban was harboring Osama Bin Laden and multiple terrorist training camps. The Taliban's reign of terror was put down and Osama Bin Laden was chased into the caves. The next target of his "war on terror", as defined by President Bush, was -- (wait for it) -- Iraq. The United States used intelligence based on out-of-date information, unsubstantiated rumors and direction from the administration to make the case that Saddam was re-arming his country and had gotten possession of weapons of mass destruction. Early in 2003, the United States finally took control of Iraq, which was the presidents' goal all along.

To date, the United States has yet to find weapons of mass destruction anywhere in Iraq. And much of the original evidence Bush based his invasion on has been proven to be false.

More specifically, any direct connection between Osama Bin Laden and Saddam Hussein has never been made. But, can there be any doubt that Iraq was a sponsor of terrorism? Not likely. Additionally, could the War on Terror ever be declared victorious with Saddam Hussein in control of Iraq? Again, the answer is most likely no.

If there are any lessons to be learned from World War II, they are that the world must see the warning signs and react before it is too late. When the world failed to keep Hitler in check, millions paid the price. When the United States failed to properly respond to the warning signs from Osama Bin Laden, thousands lost their lives. When the world failed to remove Saddam Hussein from power, hundreds of thousands lost their lives. What more evidence is needed to prove that the results we achieved in Iraq are of great importance and validity?

But the damage to America's reputation among the international community will take decades to rehabilitate. There will probably be places where the perception of the "evil America" created by these actions will never be overcome, no matter what we do. The fact is, by waging war under false pretenses we increased the number of enemies to America and decreased the security of Americans worldwide.

"Great is the guilt of an unnecessary war."

~ John Adams

U.N. Peace Keeping or "Un-Peacekeeping"

The big question is how long we will allow global security to be subverted by the inaction of the United Nations before the United States takes action. The UN has proven to have a real issue when it comes to enforcing its own resolutions or holding its members accountable for their actions. While both France and Germany signed the UN sanctions against Iraq, they were both making back door deals to harvest Iraq's oil. While the UN touted the greatness of the "Oil for Food" program, the Secretary General, Kofi Annan, knew that Saddam was using the program to make millions and divert those funds to re-arm Iraq; much as Hitler re-armed Germany. Yet, Mr. Annan, as leader of the UN did nothing to stop it. Meanwhile the Iraqi people starved. While human rights are being violated around the world, some the worst offending countries are allowed to sit as the head of the human rights council in the UN. The current actions and philosophies of the United Nations would do nothing in deterring the actions of a future Adolph Hitler. Instead, the current UN policies would serve as motivation for a future dictator to disregard all threats and resolutions -- and once again seek world domination.

I want to be very clear here; I believe strongly in the concept and charter of the United Nations as an institution. But I am gravely concerned it is not living up to the ideals it is supposed to stand for. This must be addressed. The lessons of the past are clear to all if we will choose to remove our political bias and see them for what they are. We cannot allow political affiliations to place our country in harm's way again. While disagreement about how to spur on the economy and solve other domestic problems continue, we must all come to the conclusion that the best defense is to see the warning signs and remove the threat once it has violated the rules, but well before it's too late.

The invasion of Iraq has been almost 8 years ago now and we just announced the final troop withdrawal this year. I have been thinking about and researching this action for a long time. I still believe that it was the right decision to go into Iraq but I am convinced more than ever that we went in under false pretenses. This will be something that history must decide, and those who are much better suited than I, will determine the final assessment. However, what I do know is that the world is a better place without Saddam. Yet, it troubles me greatly that members of the United Nations are not being held accountable for their back door deals with Mr. Hussein, and that there are those in this country who still believe that America did no wrong in making the case for invasion.

I wonder what does more damage; a president and administration who decide to do what they want no matter the cost to the country, or the representatives of the nations of the world standing by hoping that history will not repeat itself. It seems to me like we all need to take a good long look at our actions and be honest about what we see.

One of the costs of our freedom is that the United States must do what the American people know to be right, even if it means that the whole world will turn against her. We must lead the way because we are the only force on the planet that has the ability to put a man like Saddam down, before he morphs into a Hitler like persona. This job is left to us, and if we are not liked for it, so be it. But first we must be "bullet-proof" in the facts we present as our justification and 100% clear in stating our motivations to proceed.

A couple of points need to be made before moving on to other costs of freedom. First, we should be careful in condemning the actions we took in Iraq by using the term "war of choice". Every war is a war of choice! We did not have to go after Hitler. We could have gone after Japan, or we could have even told both powers that if they do not attack us again we will stay out of the battle altogether. We did not have to revolt against the mother country, and we could all be speaking the Queen's English today. We could have told Osama that we won't support Israel and that if he left us alone, that we would stay out of the Middle East. Yes, it was a war of choice, just like every other war! But the real choice we seemed to have a problem with was the one made by Bush and his administration not to tell us the truth about his intentions regarding the invasion of Iraq. I know it is difficult, but that should not take away from the importance of the military action and its results.

Now, let's explore the idea of "pre-emption." This term has always bothered me when it is used to describe the attack on Iraq. It is true that Iraq never attacked America, either in the 1991 Gulf War or as part of 9/11. So why don't people think of "Gulf 1" as being pre-emptive? Because ever since the end of WWII we have had a treaty with Saudi Arabia to provide the kingdom with protection for a partnership (ARAMCO- Arab American Oil Company) to develop their oil fields and ensure a cheap supply of petroleum to the U.S.. After he invaded Kuwait, Saddam made militarily moves that showed he intended to invade the Saudi Kingdom next. We were obligated to defend the Saudi's under a treaty and we were asked to provide help by the King. We did what we had to do.

So why do I believe the 2003 invasion doesn't qualify as pre-emptive? Because a) Saddam was in clear and flagrant violation of the terms of the 1991 cease-fire, b) in violation of UN resolutions, and c) guilty of corrupting the Oil for Food program. And, if that is not enough, under his orders the Iraqi military had repeatedly fired upon our service men and women stationed in the region to enforce the terms of the cease-fire "No Fly Zones" and resulting UN sanctions. Saddam fired the first shots. We lagged in our response, and Bush misled the world, but we acted completely within the rules. So I would ask you, was it a pre-emptive strike to attack Iraq or was it an enforcement of the original cease-fire agreement? You see, when Saddam signed that agreement, he gave us permission to take him out if he did not follow it. Well guess what, he didn't follow it at all. Although a ban on weapons of mass destruction was a key component of this agreement, there were many other requirements. Saddam never complied with a single one of them; much like Hitler.

One of the other arguments I hear is that the U.S. should not meddle in the internal policies of other countries by espousing things like regime change. But, the U.S. and many other governments have been doing this for hundreds of years and have been mostly successfully. The system in place has always required a joint resolution of Congress prior to taking action. This time it was no different. Congress passed a resolution authorizing and justifying this action. And most of Congress voted for, and signed, the document. In it is clearly stated:

> "Whereas the Iraq Liberation Act (Public Law 105-338) expressed the sense of Congress that it should be the policy of the United States to support efforts to remove from power the current Iraqi regime and promote the emergence of a democratic government to replace that regime..."

But you should know that it was President Bill Clinton who signed the Iraq Liberation Act promoting regime change. And any politician who tells you, that when they signed this document, they were not in support of regime change is a liar; or they did not read what they signed, which wouldn't surprise any of us.

The bottom line is that the war on Iraq should not be categorized as a "pre-emptive" "war of choice" solely for "regime change" as it has been. This is what we are being told by those do not quite understand the facts of the situation. These folks know in their hearts that the story we were told did not pass the "smell test" for some reason but were not sure why. And they are justifiably outraged by their sense that America did not live up to the ideals that created this country by engaging in this action. Their hearts are in the right place but their heads do not have all the facts. And sadly, few of the journalists we have asked to report the facts to us from the media have given us the whole story. Reporters chose not to challenge the "official" story and looked deeper for the truth. In fact, it seems to me like the media outlets could be considered a kind of co-conspirator by giving bias to the administration's party line when making decisions regarding how they covered the war. But can you blame them? After all, news coverage of a war zone has got to be better for business than reporting on the latest person kicked off "Dancing with the Stars", doesn't it?

I must study politics and war that my sons may have liberty to study mathematics and philosophy. My sons ought to study mathematics and philosophy, geography, natural history and naval architecture, navigation, commerce and agriculture, in order to give their children a right to study painting, poetry, music, architecture, statuary, tapestry, and porcelain.

~ John Adams, letter to Abigail Adams, 1780

I do believe that a strong case can be made that there were many critical mistakes, and possible criminal conspiracy, leading up to the Iraqi war. However, that does not change the fact that the attack on Iraq was necessary and within our right. I also believe that there is enough criticism to go around regarding nations that contributed to the need to invade Iraq. President Bush deserves a majority of the blame for propagating a fraud on the U.S. citizens and the world. But 'we the people' have allowed the actions of his administration to go challenged. I strongly believe that if President Bush sought to try to defend his positions today, no one would be able to "mis-underestimate" what his true motives and intentions were.

Summary

We live in dangerous times and can never forget the evil that exist in the world. Certainly, we must do better in our foreign relations, and we need to be more consistent in how we interact with others on the international stage. We need to establish a "global neighbor" policy that we are comfortable with presenting to the rest of the world and stick to it. We absolutely must become more energy efficient to ensure we do not become obliged to unstable dictators or allied with unfriendly governments. We need to understand that no matter what we do, this nation will always be a target because of who we are and what we represent to other nations around the world. We can never let our guard down, and we must always be willing to defend ourselves when and if the situation demands it. But we cannot let those who are elected to represent us mislead the public for nefarious reasons or for their own personal agenda. We should hold all those in government to the highest possible ethical standards in both international relations and domestic policy. We must also remember to look to the lessons of history and not repeat the mistakes of the past. But perhaps the greatest cost we must be willing to pay is to speak up when we discover that we have done something we shouldn't have and do whatever it takes to make things right.

5.
CALCULATING THE CONSEQUENCES

"The happy Union of these States is a wonder; their Constitution a miracle; their example the hope of Liberty throughout the world."

~ *James Madison*

--- ✦✦✦ ---

Everything in this life has consequences. Think about it. Every decision you make potentially has an effect on something or someone. Everything you do has the possibility to effect not just you, but those around you. You can affect people consciously, unconsciously or subconsciously. You could have an effect on someone and not even know it. And those effects have consequences. Potentially, every word we speak or gesture we make can have very real consequences on the world around us. It is a little scary if you stop and think about it. Not to mention the possible consequences that other peoples actions might have on us. Including those in our government.

When our government passes a piece of legislation or creates a new social program, those actions have profound consequences. -- Social Security, Unemployment Insurance, Medicare and Medicaid -- These programs have fundamentally changed the lives of every citizen of this country. Some of those changes, or consequences, have been good. Other consequences have not been so good.

Examples of the good consequences these programs have provided are numerous and easy to find: Social Security has helped millions of Americans enter their twilight years with dignity and grace. Medicare and Medicaid have helped families take care of our aging loved ones, and those with disabilities, by minimizing the financial impact of medical treatment. Unemployment Insurance provides a bridge to manage work place transitions. I am sure that everyone reading these words could give an example of the positive impact one of these programs has provided to a member of their own family.

Examples of the negative consequences these programs have are somewhat less readily available but nonetheless just as real in their impact on us all. The biggest and most obvious being the financial burden they place on the country as a whole via taxes. A less obvious consequence is one that I have stated often in this book -- that our government does not have the authority to provide these programs. And by doing them anyway, they only serve to weaken our founding documents. They also give precedent to more extra-constitutional programs that some future politician may wish to implement.

So, if creating these programs had profound consequences on this country what would the consequences of eliminating them be? In a word; Catastrophic. So, what do we do?

I personally believe we need to amend our constitution to include these fundamental programs and possibly one or two others like Universal Health-care. Why? Because programs like Social Security, Unemployment Insurance, Medicaid and Medicare represent everything that is good and right about this country. These programs offer an assistance that most people need occasionally over the course of their life. Everybody needs a helping hand now and then. I think it is an amazing country that recognizes these needs and makes that help available to its citizens.

But there is a downside to these programs. And that is the fact that they are run by huge bureaucracies that waste lots of money. Money which could be used for other things like paying off our national debt or rebuilding our crumbling infrastructure or maybe, just maybe, being left in the taxpayers pocket where it belongs.

I know there are good people out there who have a different opinion than this. They believe that these government programs are damaging to both our country and its citizens. That they cause greater harm than any good they provide. That our government should not be in the "helping hand" business. There are people who believe that simply because we have programs like "unemployment" that the vast majority of Americans will become couch potatoes and abuse the system. I do not agree.

The natural consequences of not working are clear -- they include hunger, homelessness, sickness, etc. What greater motivations could there be for going to work? I cannot think of any. These natural consequences of life, with or without various government programs, are there for a reason and are not likely to change anytime soon. To avoid these, I find it comforting to know that if I ever needed them, some small portion of the taxes I paid are available to me in an emergency situation.

For many seniors Social Security is the difference between poverty and paying the bills. Medicare/Medicaid ensures that those of us with disabilities are cared for appropriately. Unemployment insurance can literally be the difference between having the means to find new employment or falling through the cracks of society. I truly hope that the people who are against these programs never need them. But I will rest a lot easier knowing that if they ever do, they are there for them. For now.

All of these programs face serious problems we must address if we plan to keep the promises we made to our fellow citizens. And to be responsible stewards of this country, we should address those problems before we add any additional burdens to the system. For the purpose of this book, let's take a quick look at each of them.

"Information is the currency of democracy."

~ *Thomas Jefferson*

Social Insecurity

In the United States, Social Security refers to the federal "Old-Age, Survivors, and Disability Insurance" (OASDI) program. President Roosevelt signed the Social Security Act into law on August 14, 1935. The Act, which was drafted during Roosevelt's first term by the President's Committee on Economic Security, was passed by Congress as part of the New Deal. The act was an attempt to limit what were seen as dangers in modern American life, including old age, poverty, unemployment, and the burdens of widows and fatherless children. By signing this act, President Roosevelt became the first president to advocate federal assistance for the elderly.

When initially signed into law, the term Social Security covered unemployment insurance as well. The term, in everyday speech today, is used to refer only to the benefits for retirement, disability, survivorship, and death, which are the four main benefits provided by traditional private-sector pension plans.

The original Social Security Act of 1935 and the current version of the Act, as amended, encompass several social welfare and social insurance programs. The larger and better-known programs are:

~ Federal Old-Age (Retirement), Survivors, and Disability Insurance

~ Temporary Assistance for Needy Families

~ Health Insurance for Aged and Disabled (Medicare)

~ Grants to States for Medical Assistance Programs (Medicaid)

~ State Children's Health Insurance Program (SCHIP)

~ Supplemental Security Income (SSI)

~ Patient Protection and Affordable Care Act

Social Security is primarily funded through dedicated payroll taxes called the "Federal Insurance Contributions Act" tax (FICA). Tax deposits are formally entrusted to various trust funds, the best known is the "Federal Old-Age and Survivors Insurance Trust Fund". By dollars paid, the U.S. Social Security program is the largest government program in the world and the single greatest expenditure in the federal budget, with 20.8% spent for social security, compared to 20.5% spent for discretionary defense and 20.1% for Medicare/Medicaid.

The good news is Social Security is currently estimated to keep roughly 40 percent of all Americans age 65 or older out of poverty.

The Bad News

Throughout the 1950s and 1960s, during the "phase-in" period of Social Security, Congress was able to grant generous benefit increases because the system had yearly cash surpluses. For this reason,

Congressional amendments to Social Security mostly took place in even numbered years (election years) because the bills were politically popular. But by the late 1970s, this era was over. For the next three decades, projections of Social Security's finances would show large, long-term deficits, and in the early 1980s, the program flirted with immediate insolvency. From this point on, amendments to Social Security would take place in odd numbered years (years that were not election years) because Social Security reform now meant tax increases and benefit reductions. This is why Social Security became known as the "Third Rail of American Politics." Touching it meant political death.

The Social Security Trust Fund

Social Security taxes are paid into the Social Security Trust Fund maintained by the U.S. Treasury (technically, the "Federal Old-Age and Survivors Insurance Trust Fund"). The current year benefit checks are paid out from current Social Security taxes. When the amount of money coming in exceeds the amount of money going out (as they have in most years), you might think the cash balance would be left in the account. You would be wrong.

The money left over is "invested" in "special series, non-marketable U.S. Government bonds". While this may sound like a good idea, it is not. When the Social Security Trust Fund "buys" those bonds from the treasury it is indirectly financing the federal governments general-purpose spending shortfalls (i.e. covering the deficit). This means that basically the government is taking money from one account and transferring it over to a different account to pay its bills because it didn't earn enough to cover the lifestyle it has grown accustom to living.

I believe the highly technical and super nerdy accounting term used to describe this practice is known as "Robbing Peter to pay Paul".

But with respect to future debt; would it not be wise and just for that nation to declare in the constitution they are forming that neither the legislature, nor the nation itself can validly contract more debt, than they may pay within their own age, or within the term of 19 years.

~ Thomas Jefferson, September 6, 1789

In 2007, the cumulative excess of Social Security taxes and interest received over benefits paid out stood at $2.2 Trillion. But that does not mean that we have $2.2 Trillion sitting in an account somewhere, because we don't. The account is empty except for those "non-marketable" bonds. Every year, our government takes the positive cash balance generated by the FICA tax and spends it on programs and departments that it does not have enough revenue to cover. They take our tax dollars and give the trust fund those bonds as a form of I.O.U. This is a problem because those "non-marketable" Treasury securities are backed by nothing more than the "full faith and credit" of the U.S. government. This, if we read the fine print, tells us the government is only "obligated", not "liable" to repay. That means if they don't buy them back, we're stuck. Because we cannot sell "non-marketable" bonds to anyone else.

The authority, granted by Congress, to the Social Security Administration to make benefit payments extends only to its current revenues and existing Trust Fund balance (i.e., redemption of its holdings of Treasury securities). Therefore, the ability Social Security has to make full payments once annual benefits exceed revenues depends in part on the federal government's ability to make good on the bonds that it has issued to the Social Security trust fund. As with any other federal obligation, the government's ability to repay the Social Security trust fund is based on the "power to tax" and the "commitment of the Congress to meet its obligations".

Question: if our government is spending more than it is making, how does it intend to buy back these bonds from the trust?

Now, you are probably thinking; "What's the problem? I'm sure our elected representatives will do the right thing." If you are, then you have not been paying attention. Why do I think this is a possible problem? Because the last couple of paragraphs tell us that the only way we will get our money back is a) if the government raises our taxes; which is kind of like paying for something twice. Or; b) if congress feels "obligated" to do so.

I ask you to consider something before you decide if I'm Chicken Little running around claiming that the sky is falling or not. -- In 2009, the Office of the Chief Actuary of the Social Security Administration calculated an unfunded obligation of $15.1 Trillion dollars for the Social Security program. The unfunded "obligation" is the difference between the present value of the cost of Social Security and the present value of the assets in the Trust Fund and the future scheduled tax income of the program. In the Actuarial Note explaining the calculation, the Office of the Chief Actuary wrote the following:

"The term "obligation" is used in lieu of the term "liability", because liability generally indicates a contractual obligation (as in the case of private pensions and insurance) that cannot be altered by the plan sponsor without the agreement of the plan participants."

Believe it or not, The Supreme Court has already established that no one has any "legal right" to Social Security benefits. The Court decided in Flemming v. Nestor (1960) that "entitlement to Social Security benefits is not a contractual right". In this case, even though Ephram Nestor had made his payroll contributions as required, the government was able to withhold his benefits simply because they did not like his politics. He was declared a communist.

There is plenty of other case law over the years that firmly establish the precedent that even though a citizen has fulfilled his/her obligations under the rules of the program, those benefits can still be denied on an individual basis!

So what do we think will happen when the amount of FICA tax coming in does not cover the expense of the benefits that need to be paid out? What options will the governments have? How about:

A) Cut spending in other departments (like: Defense, Education, Foreign Aid, Corporate subsidies, etc.) to cover the difference

B) Cut social security benefit payouts across the board

C) Print more money to buy back the bonds from the trust

D) Look at ways to disqualify people from receiving benefits

E) all of the above.

The answer, of course, is "E". I do not believe the government will make drastic cuts to departments like Defense or cut off Foreign Aid. And I hope it does not decide to just print more money. But we have seen them already begin to freeze cost of living increases and cap benefits for Social Security. So the only thing left is to begin finding reasons to "disqualify" citizens from the program as a means of reducing the overall burden to the system. All the signs are there.

Can you imagine paying your dues and playing by the rules for 40 or 50 years, and then, when you need it most, you are told that for whatever reason you are not eligible? Don't laugh! It has happened before. More than once.

Another problem we all face is the fact that as health care has improved most of us have begun to live longer lives. This placed a strain on the program and Congress sought to relieve the problem by pushing back the age in which we can retire and begin collecting full benefits. And as a short-term solution, it worked, but it is not the answer. When the program started, in 1935, the qualifying age was 60. Today, the date you can retire is tied to the year you were born. In my case, I can retire and begin to collect the pension I have been paying into since I was a teenager once I reach age of 67. This means I still have 22 years to go before I can file for benefits.

Here is my concern: since we already know the program has problems, and since we also know one way to get short-term relief is to play with eligibility dates, my question becomes; how many more times do you think the government might push back my eligibility date in the next 22 years? No one can say for sure, but I'm willing to bet a dollar it will be at least once.

Now, the only reason I see this as an issue is that, based on the research I've seen of data compiled by the World Health Organization, Encyclopedia Britannica, Wikipedia and others reputable sources, the average life span for a person with my medical history, living where I live, with my eating habits and personal history is... 77.2 years.

So, by my calculations, if the government is not able to deny me benefits that I have earned over the better part of 52 years based on my politics, or by pushing back the age when I become eligible to after I die, then my retirement should be the best damn 5 or so years of my life! Unless, of course, they figure out a way to declare me a terrorist under the USA Patriot Act and ship me off to Gitmo. But at least there I'll get room and board (i.e. water board).

Unemployment Insurance

Unemployment compensation is money received from the United States and an individual state by a worker who has become unemployed through no fault of their own. (i.e.: did not quit, and were not fired for misconduct). It is what economists call a counter-cyclical program, pumping money into the economy when the private sector stalls. In this way, it provides insurance both for folks who lost jobs and for an economy that's lost momentum. In the United States, this compensation is classified as a type of social welfare benefit. According to the Internal Revenue Code, these types of benefits are to be included in a taxpayer's gross income when they file their federal taxes.

Federal-State Joint Programs

The idea of unemployment insurance in the United States originated in Wisconsin in 1932. In the United States, there are 50 state unemployment insurance programs plus one each in the District of Columbia, Puerto Rico and United States Virgin Islands. Through the Social Security Act of 1935, the federal government of the United States effectively encouraged the individual states to adopt unemployment insurance plans. Unemployment insurance is a federal-state program jointly financed through federal and state employer payroll taxes (federal and state UI taxes).

Generally, employers must pay both state and federal unemployment taxes if:

1) They pay wages to employees totaling $1,500 or more in any quarter of a calendar year; or,

2) They had at least one employee during any day of a week during 20 weeks in a calendar year, regardless of whether the weeks were consecutive. However, some state laws differ from the federal law.

To facilitate this program, the U.S. Congress passed the Federal Unemployment Tax Act (FUTA), which authorizes the Internal Revenue Service (IRS) to collect an annual federal employer tax used to fund state workforce agencies. FUTA covers the costs of administering the Unemployment Insurance and Job Service programs in all states. In addition, FUTA pays one-half of the cost of extended unemployment benefits (during periods of high unemployment) and provides for a fund from which states may borrow, if necessary, to pay benefits.

The amount of money a person can receive on unemployment varies in each state, but it is always a percentage of the wages they earned during a previous, established period of time. This is normally the 12-month period prior to the beginning of the most recent completed calendar quarter. Unfortunately, no matter how much money you made at your job, the maximum amount of unemployment benefits you can receive is somewhere between $300.00 and $400.00 per week, depending on your State.

I do not know about you, but that does not seem like enough money to me to even consider going without work for too long. I have belts that cost more than that.

Who pays for UI?

In normal times, states pay for up to 26 weeks of unemployment insurance with FUTA payroll tax although some states choose to provide extended benefits for up to 99 weeks. The federal government fills a "rainy day" fund and splits the cost of the extended benefits by collecting $56 per worker, nationwide. In the last two years, Washington took over the extended benefits program and as a result, further extensions to UI have been financed with deficit spending.

The Debate

There is a 'political debate' and a 'substantive debate' over unemployment insurance. In the political arena, Republicans have repeatedly blocked UI extensions because the program, which costs about $10 billion a month, adds to the deficit. Democrats and the president respond that jobless benefits should be treated like emergency disaster relief and should not require "off-setting" spending cuts or tax increases. So the political fight over UI is actually about the deficit.

This debate, in my opinion, is more philosophical than political. Both the Democrats and the Republicans seem to have forgotten that deficit spending is a bad thing. A very, very bad thing. In fact, I believe that it is immoral, unethical and irresponsible for our representatives to spend more than revenues can cover and continuously push out debt and keep doing it year after year until it reaches close to 16 trillion dollars! Seems to me they have forgotten that eventually someone is going to have to pay this bill. But since they do not plan in paying it off in their lifetime, they're under the impression that it is not their problem. We need to show them they are wrong.

The 'substantive' or policy argument against UI goes like this: Jobless insurance is a subsidy -- an incentive to stay unemployed. Somebody on UI might choose to stay unemployed longer, or hold out for better jobs, knowing he has a few hundred dollars a week holding him over. To be sure, UI might increase the unemployment rate.... slightly. The San Francisco Fed concluded that extended benefits added 0.4 percentage points to the unemployment rate nationwide. But we should also consider; a) in an economy with five unemployed for every job opening, Americans do not need unemployment benefits to discourage them from working. The job market is doing that all by itself. And b) there will always be those who abuse their freedoms (in case you forgot, see chapter 1)

Another school of thought is that unemployment insurance might even be good for the economy. The Congressional Budget Office and economist Mark Zandi of Moody's both said extending UI was one of the most effective ways to stimulate the economy in a downturn -- above even tax cuts or infrastructure spending. It puts timely money in the hands of people who are likely to spend it locally, increasing the taxable income of the people and businesses around them.

Like any government stimulus program, jobless benefits will eventually become a drag on the economy. The federal government should not, and cannot plan to subsidize two years of unemployment forever. But today, with the average unemployment duration at 29 weeks -- longer than standard state benefits -- jobless benefits are a small price to pay to keep hard-hit families, and the hard-hit economy, above water

Medicare and Medicaid

Medicare is a social insurance program administered by the United States government (CMS), providing health insurance coverage to people who are aged 65 and over; to those who are under 65 and are permanently physically disabled or who have a congenital physical disability; or to those who meet other special criteria like the End Stage Renal Disease program (ESRD). Medicare in the United States somewhat resembles a single-payer health care system but is not.

Before Medicare, only 51% of people aged 65 and older had health care coverage, and nearly 30% lived below the federal poverty level. "Original Medicare" plans (when Medicare Advantage has not been elected) cover 80% of the Medicare-approved amount of any given medical cost; the remaining 20% of cost must be paid by either a Medicare Supplement plan, which is a "supplemental insurance" from a private health insurance company (normally requiring a monthly insurance premium paid to that company by the holder), or out-of-pocket via the patient's own personal funds (check, money order, cash, etc.). Medicare Advantage plans are not Medicare Supplements but take the place of "Original Medicare". In return for a premium, these plans share costs and cap out of pocket expenses. The Medicare program also funds residency-training programs for the vast majority of physicians in the United States.

The Social Security Act of 1965 was signed into law by President Lyndon B. Johnson on July 30, 1965 as amendments to existing Social Security legislation. This legislation included the establishing of the Medicare program. At the bill-signing ceremony, Johnson enrolled former President Harry S. Truman as the first Medicare beneficiary and presented him with the first Medicare card. Truman's wife Bess got the second.

The Centers for Medicare and Medicaid Services (CMS), a component of the Department of Health and Human Services (HHS), administers Medicare, Medicaid, and various other similar programs. The Social Security Administration is responsible for determining Medicare eligibility and processing premium payments for the Medicare program.

The Chief Actuary of CMS is responsible for providing accounting information and cost-projections to the Medicare Board of Trustees to assist them in assessing the financial health of the program. The Board is required by law to issue annual reports on the financial status of the Medicare Trust Funds. Since the beginning of the Medicare program, CMS has contracted with private companies to operate as intermediaries between the government and medical providers. These contractors are commonly already in the insurance or health care area. Contracted processes include claims and payment processing, call center services, clinician enrollment, and fraud investigation.

Medicare, in the same manner as Social Security, is financed by payroll taxes imposed by the Federal Insurance Contributions Act (FICA) as well as the Self-Employment Contributions Act of 1954.

Aging of the Population

The ratio of workers paying Medicare taxes to retired people drawing benefits is shrinking, and at the same time, the price of health care services per person is increasing. Currently there are 3.9 workers paying taxes into Medicare for every older American receiving services. By 2030, as the baby boom generation retires, that is projected to drop to 2.4 workers for each beneficiary. Medicare spending is expected to grow by about 7 percent per year for the next 10 years. As a result, the financing of the program is out of actuarial balance, presenting serious challenges in both the short-term and long-term.

And Then There's Fraud

In the United States, Medicare fraud is a general term that refers to an individual or corporation that seeks to collect Medicare health care reimbursement under false pretenses. There are many different types of Medicare fraud, all of which have the same goal: to collect money from the Medicare program illegitimately.

The total amount of Medicare fraud is difficult to track, because not all fraud is detected and not all suspicious claims turn out to be fraudulent. According to the Office of Management and Budget, Medicare "improper payments" were $47.9 billion in 2010, but some of these payments later turned out to be valid. The Congressional Budget Office estimates that total Medicare spending was $528 billion in 2010. Those rough numbers mean that approximately 9% of Medicare claims are fraudulent. The Medicare program is a target for fraud because it is based on the "honor system" of billing. It was originally set-up to help honest doctors who helped the needy with medical services. There are few safeguards to eliminate false claims. In fact, claims are paid automatically because the goal of Medicare is not to root out false claims, but to pay claims quickly and smoothly.

Medicare fraud is typically seen in the following ways:

~ Phantom Billing: The medical provider bills Medicare for unnecessary procedures, or procedures that are never performed; for unnecessary medical tests or tests never performed; for unnecessary equipment; or equipment that is billed as new but is, in fact, used. In which case, every form of billing, phantom or patient, can be prevented through carefully checking.

~ Patient Billing: A patient who is in on the fraud provides his or her Medicare number in exchange for kickbacks. The provider bills Medicare for any reason and the patient is told to admit that he or she indeed received the medical treatment.

~ Upcoding scheme and unbundling Inflating bills by using a billing code that indicates the patient needs expensive procedures.

A 2011 crackdown on fraud charged "111 defendants in nine cities, including doctors, nurses, health care company owners and executives" of fraud schemes involving "various medical treatments and services such as home health care, physical and occupational therapy, nerve conduction tests and durable medical equipment."

In recent years, as regulatory requirements tightened and law enforcement has stepped up, Medicare fraud has shifted away from sectors such as durable medical equipment (items used in the home such as wheelchairs, hospital beds, nebulizers, and oxygen equipment) and HIV/AIDS infusion injections to other areas such as ambulance fraud and hospice care fraud. Durable medical equipment (or home medical equipment) now represents less than two percent of total Medicare spending. Results of the crackdown have been good which indicates that a continuous sustained emphasis should be focused on minimizing fraud in the Medicare system.

Let's Talk About the Future

Since we have come to this point, I would like to talk a little about Universal Healthcare in America. I think everyone can agree that we are living longer, healthier lives today than we were just a hundred years ago. And I think we can all agree that this is a good thing. Right? This is primarily because of advances in medicines, medical treatment breakthroughs and our access to doctors. Many, many studies have shown that the greater access to health-care professionals and the latest medicines equals a greater quality of life for a longer period of time. So, having a universal health care system in this country seemed like a "no brainer" to me. I kept asking myself "Why wouldn't we want this?" and I kept hearing people I respected from all levels of society respond with strong opinions against a national health care program. I thought I must have been missing something, so I began looking into this debate.

As a point of clarification, it is my position that the "Health care system" in the United States is mis-labeled. This is because from my perspective, what we have is not "Healthy" nor "Caring" or what I call a working "System". You can find literally thousands of examples of what I mean by watching one of the many documentaries available, visiting any number of medical information sites on the inter-net, or just by talking to friends and co-workers. I was shocked by the stories I read and the amount of information I found.

I sat on the fence about this subject for a long time because I did not feel like I had enough information to make an informed decision. When I finally decided to stop complaining about "things" and write this book, I felt strongly that I had to include a section on health care. This meant now was the time to start educating myself on the various "pro's and con's" of the universal health care debate and take a stand one way or another. I began by looking critically at the specific arguments folks had for supporting or opposing this legislation and seeking out rebuttals for both. Here, listed in no particular order, are the main arguments for and against a universal health care system and the position I have taken on each one.

Argument #1 -- "It's the first step towards Socialism"

Is it "socialism" to provide Social Security and medical benefits to all American retirees? No. What about universal free education through high school? Also, No. Or the interstate highway system, sanitation, police protection? No. No. And No. All of these are paid for by taxes, which represent a kind of "interest payment" on the huge accomplishments of Americans who have gone before us and who created the benefits and institutions we enjoy today. To me this argument is non-sequitur.

Argument #2-- "I don't want Universal Health Care because it's socialized medicine."

Universal health-care itself is not socialized medicine, which refers to medicine that is both financed and delivered by the government. In other words, the government pays for and owns the health-care system. That is the case for so-called "national health services" such as the health-care systems of Great Britain and Spain, but it is not the case for other health care systems such as in Japan, Canada, and the rest of Europe. Single-payer systems such as Canada are not socialized medicine in the sense that the mechanisms of delivery are mostly private (i.e. physicians exist mostly in the private sector).

In the U.S., unless we moved to a national health service, any UHC solution would definitely not be socialized medicine. Using an employer mandate, for example, would build on the current system of predominantly private delivery. Adopting a single payer system in this country would change only the financing mechanism of our health-care system, not the delivery mechanisms, which would stay private.

Argument #3-- "I don't want to lose control of health care decision making:"

If UHC reform passes, some bureaucrat might be able to dictate what care you can get, standing between you and your doctor. This may well be the most widespread and pernicious of all the dumb arguments against health-care reform. It certainly has some intuitive appeal, as long as you do not think about it for more than three or four seconds. Who wants some snotty bureaucrat telling my doctor what to do? That would be awful!

So true -- you would never want a government bureaucrat getting between you and your doctor. Much better to have your care controlled by an entire team of insurance-company bureaucrats, whose bonuses and promotions depend on denying your claims and limiting your care. That is, if you have a plan in the first place, what with their denial of your pre-existing conditions and their attempts to kick you off your policy if you actually get sick. That is so much better than letting some government bureaucrat get involved.

Argument #4-- "It's the uninsured fault that they're uninsured"

Is it really anyone's fault that health insurance is so expensive that they cannot afford it? The high costs of health care are due to influences beyond any one individual's control - they are influenced by society-wide trends towards increased use of technology, high administrative costs of our health-care system, and a strong profit motive in the health insurance industry that drives up the cost of premiums. 8 out of 10 of the uninsured work or come from working families. They play by the rules, work hard just like the rest of Americans, and yet they cannot get insurance from their employer because it is not offered, or they cannot afford it if it is offered. Is that their fault?

Argument #5-- "The uninsured should take more individual responsibility to get insurance. It's not our responsibility to give them insurance".

A small percentage of the uninsured can afford insurance but choose not to obtain it. Most of these are young, healthy individuals. Should these people go to the ER or become hospitalized, their medical bills may become so great that they can't afford to pay them, in which case the hospital often writes off all or part of their bill as "uncompensated care." In so doing, government and individuals with private insurance end up subsidizing the cost of care for these people, who essentially become "free-riders" off the system.

For the vast majority of the uninsured, however, inability to afford health insurance, and not a conscious choice, is the reason they are uninsured. It is fine to say that people should take individual responsibility if they can afford to carry out that responsibility. Since this is not the case for the majority of the uninsured, it becomes ridiculous to argue that the problem of un-insurance can be solved with simple individual responsibility.

Argument #6— "The uninsured are lazy and free-ride off the health care system — why should I care about them?"

If we had a system of universal health-care, in which all Americans were able to access the health-care system when needed, there would be no need for uncompensated care. This should appeal both to those who dislike free riding as well as to the uninsured, most of whom don't have any other choice but to take advantage of uncompensated care.

Argument #7-- "Universal health-care would essentially be a government handout to the uninsured."

Universal health-care would result in a number of moral, economic, and cultural benefits. It is not a welfare policy for the uninsured; rather, it is a policy whose benefits would accrue to all Americans. For example, universal health-care would save money, improve our health, and create a society with more equal opportunity. These are things all Americans can enjoy and should find agreeable.

Education is something that is provided by the government. Is education a handout to society? Or is it a wise policy that makes America stronger? Many services are provided by the government that can be seen as "handouts." Corporate welfare (e.g. the subsidization of oil companies by the government through tax breaks and direct subsidies) might be considered a government handout, depending on one's political perspective.

Argument #8-- "Everyone who is uninsured can get Medicaid, so what's the problem?"

This is a myth. The federally defined minimum group of eligible individuals includes poor children and pregnant women, as well as VERY poor parents and elderly/disabled individuals. Many poor people make too much money to qualify for Medicaid, and childless adults (who constitute over half of the uninsured) do NOT qualify for Medicaid. States do have the option of expanding Medicaid eligibility beyond the federally defined eligibility guidelines in some cases, but childless adults are not covered by Medicaid under any state.

Argument #9-- "We have the best health care system in the world. Why should we endanger it by adopting universal health care?"

There is no way to measure objectively which health-care system is the best in the world. America, however, certainly does not measure up well against other countries on many health indicators. For example, our life expectancy lags behind that of other countries, and our infant mortality rate is higher than that of other countries. The World Health Organization ranks our health-care system 37th on overall performance, and 24th on health level attainment. All of these mediocre performance measures are unacceptable, especially given that we spend almost twice as much per capita on health-care than any other country.

It is true that America offers some of the best care in the world; for those who can afford it. We would in fact have one of the best health-care systems in the world if we were able to allow everyone to access and afford that high-quality care.

Argument #10-- Healthcare is not a right.

Even if healthcare is not a right, universal healthcare might still be the wisest public policy because of its moral, economic, and cultural benefits. Education is not defined in our Constitution as a right. Yet, the vast majority of Americans support the idea that everyone should have access to public education. How is healthcare different?

Argument #11-- No one should get free healthcare.

There's no such thing as free healthcare anywhere in the world. Every system has some sort of cost-sharing and/or fails to covers some service, especially things like dental care. Moreover, every healthcare system is financed by taxes to some degree, so nothing is really "free." If the purpose of a healthcare system is to maximize health, then it makes sense to align financial incentives such that people will utilize the most effective, low-cost interventions. For instance, primary care visits are more cost-effective than ER care or being hospitalized for conditions that could have been prevented through good primary care. Making primary care visits free or extremely low cost removes a major barrier to seeking out such care and therefore saves money (incidentally, the idea of making primary care visits free is not without precedent; all general practitioner (GP) visits in the UK are free at the point of service). In this sense, a wise designer of a healthcare system should in fact make certain things free or low-cost, and make less effective interventions higher cost.

Argument #12-- Healthcare should be treated like an individual commodity – it should only be available to those who can afford it.

Healthcare is a basic human need. You can live without individual commodities like a VCR or TV, but a lot of people can't live without healthcare in their everyday lives, and no one can live without healthcare when they are seriously ill. Healthcare costs are unpredictable – you never know when you are going to get sick, but you can predict when you will spend money on a VCR or TV.

Argument #13-- We can't afford UHC.

We can't afford to NOT have UHC. The Institute of Medicine estimates that over $65-$130 billion is lost each year due to lost productivity by the uninsured, who are less healthy and therefore less able to be a productive member of society. Other economic costs include a loss of global competitiveness (since companies in other countries don't bear as much of a burden in terms of health care costs), unnecessary use of the expensive ER, strain on businesses, and paying for preventable costly diseases due to lack of health care access. In 2005, The National Coalition on Health Care released a report arguing that UHC would save at least $320 billion over 10 years under four different scenarios, with a single payer system saving $1.1 trillion over 10 years.

Argument #14-- UHC would create waiting lists.

There already is an infinite waiting list for people who are uninsured in America. To argue that there aren't already waiting lists in America flies in the face of reality – it often takes months to get an appointment with specialists and even primary care physicians, especially if you are a new patient to that physician. Other countries that have UHC and waiting lists do not spend nearly as much as America does on health care. Waiting lists in America would be significantly less of a problem because of this spending. Waiting lists in other industrialized countries are almost always for elective surgeries and procedures – no country has a waiting list for emergency procedures, and virtually no country has waiting lists for primary care visits.

Argument #15— "UHC would result in the rationing of care."

Health care is a scarce resource, and EVERY country in the world therefore has to find some sort of mechanism for rationing. In other countries, health care is rationed according to need, whereas in this country, health care is rationed according to the ability to pay. We already ration in this country! In other countries, the discussion about whom to prioritize for health care, what procedures to pay for, etc. is fundamentally a public, democratic process. In this country, these discussions are made in the board rooms of big businesses (the private health insurance companies) and are therefore fundamentally not democratic.

Argument #16-- Jobs will be lost during the transition from our current system to UHC.

All reform is difficult, no matter what it is. Health care reform is no different. The question is about priorities: where there's a will for UHC, there will be a way. Even under more difficult transitions, such as with a single payer system in which the private insurance industry is minimized, the country will need people to help administer the new program. People could be transitioned from the private insurance industry to the new program. UHC will create new jobs throughout the country – right now, businesses are either firing or not hiring low-wage workers because of health insurance costs, and many people stay with their current jobs just to get health insurance benefits instead of starting their own businesses.

Argument #17-- "What's mine is mine"

There is a fundamental argument against a UHC health plan that is not being openly expressed in polite company yet. Let's personalize this discussion to keep it realistic. It goes like this;

'I believe that if I have a "material super-abundance" and someone else has a basic "material need" he cannot supply for himself, then that other person has some kind of claim on me. (Note that I say "need" and not "desire.") I cannot address that unknown person's need fairly all by myself through some act of personal charity, which, by definition, will be arbitrary. Only government guided by a national democratic process can address those needs fairly and equitably.'

So my interpretation of this argument against universal health-care comes down to: "That other person you talk about has NO claim on me. What I have is exclusively mine and to take anything from me is socialism/communism/dictatorship. If another person has needs he cannot remedy, then it is his fault or his bad luck. Don't trouble me about it."

As I see it, that is the basic point being made by most of those people using any of the above arguments against providing health services to the citizens of this country. And you know what? That's their right. As Americans, they can take any position they want. That's the beauty of the democratic system. Freedom to believe whatever you choose. Another beautiful thing about our system is the ability to use public opinion to influence policy. If enough of us demand some sort of Universal Health Care system than our elected officials better follow our lead and pass legislation providing it or we will vote them out of office. If we don't, then we won't get one. It is that simple.

All, too, will bear in mind this sacred principle, that though the will of the majority is in all cases to prevail, that will to be rightful must be reasonable; that the minority possess their equal rights, which equal law must protect, and to violate would be oppression.

~ Thomas Jefferson, First Inaugural Address, March 4, 1801

What I believe is that most people who have taken these positions have not spent much time thinking through the problem, or worse, are just repeating what they hear on the radio and TV. You cannot blame people for this. Most folks have a lot on their plates. Work, family, social commitments and all sorts of distractions have prevented most Americans from realizing the information they receive from the mainstream media has been filtered heavily based on party platforms or corporate agendas. But that, my friends, is a whole other subject.

Summary

"We the people" need to understand the consequences of our actions. We must teach our representatives fiscal responsibility. None of us can just push debt off to some unknown date, take money from a different account without repercussions or just print more money whenever we feel like it. We are placing a burden on future generations who are going to be stuck paying off the debts we created. What are we saying when we choose to do this? The answer; that we have created problems we do not know how to solve.

I, for one, believe that what we do is much more important than what we say. And what we are doing is telling the world and those future generations that we only care about ourselves. That we are living only for today. That we think we are more important than anybody else, including our children and grandchildren, and that we are just plain incapable of doing the right thing.

That is not a legacy I feel comfortable leaving behind.

I believe we can fix this mess. "Yes", it will come down to some very hard choices, and "No", it is not going to be easy. But we know what we need to do. And we damn sure know that we cannot leave it up to the folks in Washington D.C.

Situations like this are guaranteed not to make either side happy. And it is a pretty safe bet that we will fight about the specific "how" we go about righting this ship. I just hope we can find common ground and at least agree on the "why" -- because we all know it is the right thing to do.

We must reign in federal spending. We must look at cutting back on some of the programs currently in place as a short-term way of freeing up capital. We have to look at every single department and program currently under administration by the federal government, and then overhaul them, so they become more efficient in their operations and more conservative in their spending. We no longer have the luxury of choosing whether we can fix this problem through spending cuts or increased taxes. It is going to require both. And it is going to have a serious impact on everyone. But really, what other choice do we have?

6.
THE VALUE OF BEING AMERICAN

The Sun never shined on a cause of greater worth.

~ Thomas Paine, Common Sense, 1776

This chapter may seem a little out of place in a book that is supposed to be about the cost associated with democracy. But I think it is important for everyone to understand that paying a price for something indicates a belief that what you are buying has value. Our founding fathers knew this. They understood the value of life, liberty and the ability to pursue happiness. They risked everything for these principles. These men were labeled traitors, had their property seized, even fought and died to pay for the freedoms we enjoy today. If they had not been successful, the cost they would have had to pay is hard for us to imagine.

One of the problems we face as a nation today is that a majority of Americans have never been asked to pay a price to be American. Being born in this day and age has brought about a sense of entitlement, an over-inflated sense of self-worth and a lack of understanding regarding the price that past generations have paid to ensure American principles endure. Our generation needs to ask ourselves some hard questions like; "What is the value of being an American?" and, "If being an American really does have value, then what is the cost we need to pay?" and finally, "Are we willing to pay it?" I truly hope we are.

Calculating Market Value

To determine the value of being American, we first need to discuss American "values". Values can be defined as those things that are important to an individual, organization or a country like broad preferences concerning appropriate courses of action or specific outcomes. As such, values reflect a person or a country's sense of right and wrong or even what "ought" to be. "Equal rights for all ", "Excellence deserves admiration", and "People should be treated with respect and dignity" are representative of values.

One place where values are important is in relation to vision. The vision of our founding fathers was clear. They included such beliefs as; "Freedom", "Democracy", "Equality", "Self Determination", "Champion of the little guy", "Helper of the Oppressed" and "Defender against Tyranny". Some of the other values that have become ingrained in our national self-definition over the past two and a half centuries are; "Capitalism", "Strength", "Manifest Destiny", "Freedom of Religion", "Family" and "Personal Wealth". These "values ", right or wrong, have become how we, and the rest of the world, view America as a nation.

Now, even a casual reader of these can see where conflicts could arise among them. "Capitalism" and "Strength" have made America what we are today, but they have generated their own set of inequalities and international resentments. "Equality" is a wonderful ideal, but frankly, not everyone is treated equal in society today. "Freedom" is fine until we see the damage caused by our vast money-obsessed entertainment apparatus who assault us with base immorality, biased news, and stupidity based programming.

But "value definitions" like these are subjective and will be influenced by those we associate with. I am positive people in the entertainment industry do not feel like freedom is a bad thing and I am sure there are people out there who think capitalism has done nothing wrong. It is all in our perception of these characteristics. But I think it is safe to say "values" are neither universal nor inherent. If that were true, we would not have political parties or some of the issues we face today.

Now, if we are to believe the propaganda being spread by these political parties, then we would have to agree that America's current "values" seem divided fairly equally between the "Liberal" and "Conservative" camps. These groups rigidly define themselves then try to convince their members that they alone are on the side of righteousness. It seems pretty obvious to me that these parties serve no other purpose than to divide us. As President Washington stated in a previous chapter, the way these party's work is by distorting and misrepresenting their opposition's positions in order to convince you to follow them. Also, as President Washington astutely pointed out, that even under the best of circumstances and with the most honorable of intentions, the natural course of party politics is that the parties will eventually end up putting their own priorities ahead of the countries, or the people's, in order to win elections. It is simply human nature; everyone wants to be on the winning team, and will do just about anything to make that happen. In my opinion, these party people, both on the right and left, are the number one cause of corruption to the democratic process this nation is facing today. This is because the more hard-core members of these groups are the ones who have dedicated their lives to partisan politics. They became the principle philosophical drivers of party platforms and the ones who are willing to fight to the death to see their opposition lose rather than America win.

As an example, over the last twenty-five years or so, the most radical members of the right wing have claimed they have owned the core American values that I have just enumerated; moreover, they have claimed that liberals are actively trying to defeat them. Therefore, they argue, liberals are trying to ruin the American way of life. They claim that liberals are a threat to our very future. If you question this assumption, you need only to tune in to AM talk radio, watch Fox news or listen to the Republican leadership to see my point. The left wing is not any better. They let these types of statements go unchallenged. Then the radical left gives speeches or proposes legislation that gives these arguments some validity without disputing the fact that they are engaging in the politics of division just as much as the right. What makes this situation so untenable is these are our "elected representatives". They are the people who pass for responsible voices in our system today.

Folks, I am going to let you in on their dirty little secret: These parties gain their identity from imagined enemies. Because without these imagined enemies, these parties are not viable. There can be no 'Hero' unless there is a 'Villain'. Without imagined enemies, you just have - other Americans.

Obviously, we are Americans struggling with competing interests among our core values. Should we try to help the poor while building wealth for us all; Should we try to lead the world without exploiting or dominating it; Should we not be ashamed of our faith in God and still try not to discriminate against those of different beliefs; and should we try to figure out balances between those "right and left" policy disputes, such as protection of the environment versus encouraging development. My answer is "Absolutely".

This is the true American value: We are a nation of compromises. The Constitution is a document of concessions between competing interests. We weigh the right of the accused against the power of prosecutors; we weigh the power of Congress against the President; we weigh the power of the people against the strength of the government. And like anything else, the scales we use need adjustment from time to time.

What we have seen recently is the creation of a culture of hate in America. I don't believe this is too strong of a characterization or a misrepresentation. Today, the radicals of both parties actually try to vilify those who disagree with them - it is the only way they can survive. For without their enemies (that they themselves imagine), they are nothing. And after the imagined enemies are all gone, they will have nothing left to rant against, except the notion of American values. Therefore, in their minds, if they lose their "enemies", they have lost America. In my opinion, this is where the future of America is most threatened, and we must fight them at every turn.

America is a balancing act. Sure, sometimes we slip off the wire. No one ever said it was going to be easy and no one ever promised us it would be simple. America is now, and will always be, a work in progress. The real danger to America is when we allow those who vilify any of our basic American values to have the loudest voices or have the last word.

I know of no safe depository of the ultimate powers of the society but the people themselves; and if we think them not enlightened enough to exercise their control with a wholesome discretion, the remedy is not to take it from them but to inform their discretion.

~ Thomas Jefferson

Retail v. Wholesale Value

In my frame of thinking, we must each look at the value of our citizenship through a prism. A prism breaks down the spectrum of light into various facets, which are connected to each other, yet are also separate and unique. This is the way we need to look at the value we receive, and the cost we must pay, to be Americans. We, as Americans, pride ourselves on being uniquely individual yet we understand that we are all connected and dependent on one another as a society. When you add to that the layers of depth we must consider as we look at our commitment, our ability and our desire to pay that price, it is easy to see how the scales can get out of balance.

Each one of us has to believe in, and place a value on, their own citizenship. For example, one person may choose to align themselves with a particular party or candidate and spend time volunteering to register voters or passing out information, while another person might decide only to show up on election day and cast a vote. Still another person might choose to give up personal privacy and run for public office. Does this mean that they each place a different value on being American? Does the person who commits more time and effort deserve a greater share of democracy than the person who only shows up to vote? The answer is "No".

Each one has chosen to participate in the process in the way that works best for them. Each will see the results of that participation, and each will have done their duty as Americans. That is how the system works. Freedom means having the ability to determine for yourself just how much involvement is required from you while keeping in mind the responsibility we all share to each other, to our ancestors and to our descendants. No American is entitled to "more" freedom than any other American. What if that person who only showed up to vote turned out to be firefighter who, after risking his life all day, just didn't have enough energy to go canvassing for voters?

I will suggest to you that if there is anyone who could reasonably be considered as entitled to an "extra share" of freedom, it would be the members of the United States Armed Forces. Why? Because no one, repeat; NO ONE has placed a higher value on their citizenship than the person who has enlisted in our active military and swears an oath to defend this nation even with their life. There is just no greater price one can pay.

Our Soldiers today are an amazing and inspiring group of young men and women who endure hardship and struggle with a pride of service that is second to none. Their Military Commanders are some of the most dedicated, educated and honorable folks to put on the uniform in all of human history. These people have made a conscience decision to dedicate a portion of their lives to serving a greater good by putting themselves in harm 's way in order to defend this nations values. I ask you: Is there anyone out there who can compete with that?

The men and woman of our all-volunteer military take on this responsibility for low pay, no recognition and few tangible benefits. And, they do it to protect complete strangers! Over the last few years, I have had the privilege of meeting hundreds of these "Hero's" serving in the military today and I must tell you that I am in "AWE" of these truly great American citizens and the sacrifices they are willing to make on my behalf. A soldier in the U.S. Military shows us what "Value" (with a capital V) true Americans are willing to place on their citizenship.

Let each citizen remember at the moment he is offering his vote that he is not making a present or a compliment to please an individual - or at least that he ought not so to do; but that he is executing one of the most solemn trusts in human society for which he is accountable to God and his country.

~ *Samuel Adams, in the Boston Gazette on April 16, 1781*

Shoplifting Citizenship

It is the person who doesn't show up to vote at all that concerns me greatly. Estimates ranges from 40 - 70% of eligible voters do not participate during midterm elections and the experts say that number does not improve much during the Presidential campaign season. Approximately 35 - 50% of eligible Americans voters cast their ballots every four years. What is the other 50 - 65% thinking? By not participating, they are essentially "free-riding" on the system and basically "shoplifting" their citizenship. And, just like an actual shoplifter, when someone free rides someone else has to pick up the tab.

Being American is our birthright and every American is, and should always be, considered equal under the law. As such, we cannot even think about imposing "levels of citizenship" based on how much a person chooses to participate in the process. That would not only be unconstitutional, it is just plain un-American. We need to make participating in our governmental processes something everyone engages in gladly. We, as American citizens, should feel a true "pride of ownership" in doing everything possible to make this experiment in democracy a success and it should be unacceptable to do anything less. If we choose not to do our part, or sit back and let our friends and neighbors blow off their responsibility, than we are just as guilty as they are and should be ashamed for being "enablers."

What does it say about us as a nation when we sit back and let up to half of our fellow citizens get away with not participating? The American people should be embarrassed if over 5% of the eligible voters do not come out to cast a ballot on Election Day. We might even think about not allowing the results of an election that did not have at least a 90% participation rate to be certified. Now that could have some interesting consequences!

No Deposit/No Return

I have been stunned by the number of good honest people I've met around the country who told me that they chose not to vote primarily due to a feeling that one vote doesn't make a difference one way or another, or, that they believe one politician is just the same as another. They believe it really makes no difference who wins the election. I have even had folks tell me they are attempting to undermine the system by not participating. I sometimes wish I could grab these people by the shoulders and shake some sense into them, but I don't. I usually just try to explain a few fundamental flaws in their logic and hope I get through. I'm not always certain I do.

I will say that I have noticed a disturbing common thread amongst these groups and that is it seems quite a few of the people who hold these opinions are the same ones who complain the loudest about specific government policies and/or politicians in general. I have a phrase I use when I notice this happening. I look them in the eye and say; "No Deposit/No Return" and then change the subject.

This is my way of saying I believe that since they did not indicate what they wanted by not participating, then they should not be upset with what they got. For this reason, I do not have a lot of patients and I am not willing stand there and listen to them complain. I try not to be too harsh about how I go about it, but I feel strongly about this, so folks usually get my point. After they do, then I try to show them the error in their logic and try to convince them to give the process one more chance.

Democracy, and Freedom for that matter, is like the old glass bottles I used to collect as a kid. I didn't know it at the time, but they taught me a valuable lesson about life and the value of things. The reason I collected them to begin with was they were worth money. Back then, when you bought a soft drink you paid a "deposit" of a nickel for the glass bottle it came in. Those bottles were ahead of their time because they were one of the first recycled containers. They would be collected and returned to the store that would send them back to the manufacturer where they would be cleaned, refilled and sold again. The only way the manufacturer could be reasonably be sure they would get the bottles back is by charging you a deposit. People used to have wooden crates on their back porches or inside their garages where they would keep their empty pop bottles until they got around to returning them to the store. As a kid, whenever my friends and I needed money for something, we would go around, collect stray bottles, and return them for a nickel a piece.

Return on Investment

In my own way, I learned that anything that has value requires an investment. Those bottles looked like trash, but nobody threw them away. And most people had special places around their homes where they set them aside. Folks new that when they bought their soda pop that they not only had the product they purchased, but a piece of company property as well. And that if they took care of it and returned it, there was a payoff in the end. This is the message I try to share with the (far too) many Americans who have chosen not to vote and therefore not have their voices heard in forging the future of this country. And, I truly hope by telling you this story that I haven't come across as some weird, nostalgic old guy with a bottle fetish, but rather someone who really cares about this country and the people who live here.

<u>Caveat Emptor</u>

Something to keep in mind; as this book is going into the finishing touches prior to printing I was made aware of a proposed law that just made its way onto the Senate floor. Right now, there is pending legislation (S 1698, the "Enemy Expatriation Act") which will give the federal government authorization to revoke the citizenship of any American. -- Yes, you read that right.

This proposed new law offers apparently innocent amendments and additions to a piece of existing federal legislation known as Title 8. Title 8 "...outlines the role of aliens and nationality in the U.S. Code." The Enemy Expatriation Act is just one small piece of the massive and complex law that is Title 8 and seeks to modify Section 349, the means by which "a person who is a national of the United States whether by birth or naturalization shall lose his nationality..." This includes anyone voluntarily "engaging in, or purposefully and materially supporting, hostilities against the United States...."

To be sure, most of us would be in favor of revoking American citizenship if it has been improperly, perhaps surreptitiously attained by terrorists who have entered the United States to commit acts of violence and murder.

But it is necessary to remember that we are dealing with Washington, DC here. To the Federal Government, recent history has shown that it is folks like Libertarians, soldiers returning from combat, gun owners, and militia members, devout believers in the Constitution and those who loudly mistrust and criticize the federal government who are thought to be the true threats of "engaging in hostilities against the United States." Someday, someone in power may just decide that all 'criminals' fit this description whether they are terrorists or not. One day it could be as simple as not paying your taxes on time or even public protest and organized dissent that qualify's as 'committing a hostile act'. And that could be all that is needed to give the government reason to take away what is ours by birth and bestowed on us by our creator.

The only way to prevent this type of legislation is to participate.

Summary

Being an American has a value that is hard to put a price on. We live in a special place at a special moment in time. It does not matter what level of commitment you make, just make it. Do your part to make this a better place. We owe it to those who have paid the way before we got here, and, it's our responsibility to those who are coming later. Don't let some political machine dictate your level of involvement or distort your perception of those you disagree with. We are all Americans and have much more in common than we have differences. We have much more to lose if we follow the divisive policies of political parties and so much more to gain if we all work together as Americans. Make your investment and reap the rewards. It starts with you and ends with US.

7.
<u>SUMMARY</u>

But a Constitution of Government once changed from Freedom, can never be restored. Liberty, once lost, is lost forever.

~ John Adams, letter to Abigail Adams, July 17, 1775

Before I bring this book to a close, I thought it might be a good idea to give the reader a bit of context as to why I felt it necessary to write this personal manifesto in the first place. Bear with me as I give it my best shot:

A few years ago, I lost the love of my life, my wife Anne, to cancer. This was the woman who I had intended to spend the rest of my life with. I was shattered emotionally and went through a dark period. For a long time I shut my emotions down. I quit communicating with my family and friends, distanced myself from everything important in my life and did my best to get lost in my work. I took on demanding projects that required long hours, lots of travel and very little 'down' time. When that didn't work, I would end up in the bottom of a glass. To be honest, it was mostly about doing anything that would allow me not to deal with my loss and the emotions I was feeling.

This experience had a profound effect on me, and more importantly, how I saw the world. I spent a lot of time thinking about life and watching those around me go about the daily motions of living. I looked to see who was happy and who was not and spent a lot of time trying to figure out why. Then one day it dawned on me; a majority of people are just trying to live honest, decent lives. Yes, we all have experienced those obnoxiously happy folks out there, and, yes, we probably all know a few of the miserable bastard types. But those people are the extremes. Most folks are just trying to make the best out of the hand they have been dealt. This isn't good or bad, happy or sad; it just is what it is. Then I realized there are people out there who had been given much harder situations to deal with than I and I needed to get back in the game.

It took a lot of 'people-watching' for me to figure things out. A couple of years, actually. So much in my life had changed during the time I spent coming to terms with my loss. Somewhere along the way, I realized I was alone and miserable. To make matters worse, I realized I had no idea how I could go about changing things.

I really disliked the person I had become. This was not an easy thing for me to admit. I had always been considered one of the "good guys". Someone who, if asked, would give you the shirt off my back to help out. It was hard to come to terms with my change because, as much as I disliked who I had become, I knew I could never go back to the person I used to be. Too many things had changed. How I saw the world had changed. My priorities had changed. I had changed.

I needed to figure out who I had become, and what changes were going to be necessary for me to evolve into the kind of man I knew I was meant to be. At first, figuring out that I needed...actually wanted...to change was difficult. But, once I made the decision, the process of change was not that hard at all. It may sound cliché but I realized that, in order to succeed, I only had to change one thing; and that was... "Everything".

Probably the biggest change I made was the decision not to hold back my opinion about things. Not in a bad way. I don't go around criticizing everything I disagree with. Rather, I try to be open and honest in the most positive manner I can. My new "mantra" became; "If you are prepared to hear the truth, ask me. If you want something 'sugarcoated', eat a donut." As a joke, I tell people that I had the filter between my thoughts and my mouth surgically removed, so don't be shocked by what comes out.

Man, let me tell you, its been liberating!

I had burned more than a few bridges during what I call my "Walk-about" period, and I was not at all sure how some would respond to my coming back. So, one of the first things I did was identify those people who were important in my life and write each a letter. In it, I apologized for my actions and told each of them how grateful I was that they tried to be there for me and how I feel like I am a better person today for having them share a part of my life. That even though much has happened, and even more has changed; I was on my way back. I told them that I missed, and needed, their friendship in my life. Once back home, I went about showing them how much I cared through my actions. You see, I think that what we 'do' is much more important than what we 'say'. I would much rather show you how I think or feel than try to tell you. I am happy to report that, for the most part, almost everyone I approached was glad to see my transition back and responded well to the changes I had made. I've always been blessed with extraordinary luck.

Probably the biggest lesson I learned from everything I went through was that I would never really 100% 'get over' the losses in my life. But, I absolutely believe now that I can, and will, be able to 'get beyond' them. The 'new me' had things I wanted to say and had new goals I intended to accomplish. I think that these things are a combination of the best parts of the 'old me' mixed with the amazing influence Annie had on my life. Including the lessons, I learned during the darkest days of my walk-about. My life is good today. I still have some things I could do better, but I am at peace with myself.

As time went on, I began thinking about how to apply this concept of change to the world around me. What were the really big things I believed in? What important matters should I try to, hopefully, make a little better? Where could I channel some of the natural energy, passion and abilities I have to see about making the world a better place? As these thoughts were going through my head, I remembered a passage I once read in George Bernard Shaw's book "*Back to Methuselah*"

"*....I hear you say "Why?" Always "Why?" You see things; and you say "Why?" But I dream things that never were; and I say "Why not?"*"

I decided it was time for me to stop asking "why" and start asking "why not".

I have had an interesting career and have been lucky enough to find myself in the position to be able to talk with a some people that everybody wishes they could get a chance to chat with. (Like celebrities, politicians, businesspersons and artists) And, through the work I do with non-profit agencies, I had the opportunity to talk to some folks that nobody ever asks for their opinion. (Like the homeless, recovering addicts, people convicted of crimes that are just getting the chance to start over, etc.) After listening to what everyone had to say, and finding quite a bit of common ground, I began to discuss what I had heard with some people I thought could help. From this, I began to develop a couple of projects that I hope will be my legacy. This book is one of them.

Now, I have no delusions that I am going to change the world by writing a book about [YAWN!] politics, or with any of the other projects I am working on. But hey, at least I'm doing something!

If I am lucky enough to get one thing to come out of these pages it would be that I think this country is incredibly important. Not just to Americans, but to people of all nationalities, as an example of what could be. I also want to convey that I am convinced this country has lost its way and is on the verge of imploding. This is why I felt like I had to do something.

My goal in writing this book is to get everyone who reads these pages to take some time and consider the state this country is in today, and then determine what price we, as a society, are willing to pay to ensure our freedoms are not whittled away in the name of some watered-down version of democracy. To remind you that the privilege of being American has a cost attached. To get you to understand that there are financial costs, physical costs, civil costs, criminal costs, personal costs, public costs and even emotional costs to allowing the people, as a whole, to live in Freedom. Real freedom. Freedom to do as we will so long as our individual actions do not encroach upon the freedoms of others. That if we do things properly, and with respect, we should be allowed to live our lives and pursue our happiness as we see fit.

As I bring this book to a close, I truly hope that I have given the reader something to think about. The truth of the matter is this country has been sliding further and further away from the original intent dreamed of by the men who dared to want to live in peace and freedom 230+ years ago. If you take some time, and do just a little research, you might discover a few interesting details about how this government and our politicians have changed over the years -- not always for the better.

For instance, did you know that high political office was not intended to be a representative's only career? Today, we have politicians who appear to have been born and raised to hold office, from families with long traditions of holding office, who get upset when challenged about their "right" to hold office. The original concept of representation was those elected would go to the Capitol to propose, write and vote on legislation. Then they would go back home to run their businesses or farms until the next session. If a member of congress became a 'full-time politician' he was viewed as being 'out of touch' with the issues in his district or state, and would be voted out of office.

Campaigns used to be about issues and policy, not about personality and the 'gotcha' politics of division we have today. Governing was about action based on the will of the people, not pandering to special interest groups or trading your vote for 'pork'. Being elected to office used to be about doing what was right, not about doing whatever it takes to get re-elected. When a politician gave a speech it was supposed to be about what they truly believed, not about party 'spin' or what some pollster told them 'we the people' wanted to hear. Moreover, politicians were once judged based on their honesty and integrity, not about how much money they could raise. You can make up your own mind about how far we have strayed.

The traits listed above are just a few of the reasons why I never refer to our elected representatives as 'leaders'. I do not feel like we have had an "elected leader" in quite some time. I also believe that if, in fact, they are leading us anywhere, it is probably in the wrong direction.

As one citizen to another, I ask you to keep in mind the principles this nation was based on and to hold true to the reality that our government was never intended to be all things to all people. That no matter how tempting it may sound, we must resist the idea that we can protect freedoms by removing or limiting those freedoms we all share. We must also understand that we cannot increase the freedom of one group without diminishing the freedom of another. We must embrace the idea that one of the costs of freedom is that we might fail, and if we try to take away the ability to fail, one of the results will be that we have taken away the ability to succeed. Also, we can never forget that when it comes to the federal government, smaller is almost always better. We must never abandon the idea that the Constitution was designed to limit the power and scope of government, not to limit the freedoms of the people. A Constitution that is not upheld as the guiding framework we all agree to abide by is a document that is destined to become irrelevant. A key part of all of this is that if 'we the people' are dissatisfied with our elected officials, it is up to us to make the necessary changes via the ballot box. We cannot allow our freedoms to be whittled away in the name of tolerance, political correctness or as an emotional response to tragic circumstances even though it may sound like a good idea at the time. Free speech is the greatest weapon that we have against corruption, and if we allow controls to be placed on that speech in the name of protecting freedom, we will limit the effectiveness of this weapon. Yes, we should be courteous to others and treat them as we wish to be treated, but we should never force anyone to do so; under the penalty of law. We need to remember that our citizenship is the greatest gift that we possess in the United States, but its value has been diminished by a lack of participation and allowing a type of national apathy to overtake the process.

Finally, we absolutely must admit that our government has shortcomings. That for the most part, the federal government has failed to achieve goals like the ones mentioned above every time it has tried. Glorious failures, which spent incredible amounts of money in the process and created mountains of debt we are passing on to our children and grandchildren. We must assume responsibility for this debt now and take action to get this under control.

I have spent several months thinking, researching and documenting how I feel about the topics covered in this book, and as I said, I have listened to what many people had to say about our political system and the problems we face. A major theme I hear repeatedly is one of frustration, with an overwhelming belief that those in power have sold them out.

This, more than anything else, prompted me to begin sharing the feedback and feelings folks shared with me to a few friends and associates. We began discussing ways to try to bring the process of government back to the people and to re-engage all those who have given up or been let down. We decided that one of the best ways we can accomplish this is by forming a political action committee (PAC) of our own based upon all we had learned. We agreed that our PAC should be based on a few basic American principles and must be open to anyone, of any party, who is interested in joining us to make change. We chose the name "The League of Non-Aligned Voters" to convey this message. Please take a moment to review our ideological covenant;

LEAGUE OF NON-ALIGNED VOTERS
~ <u>IDEOLOGICAL COVENANT</u> ~

We the people, of the newly formed League of Non-aligned Voters, drawing from the diverse cultural backgrounds and wide variety of perspectives available in America today, officially express our intentions to work together in order to create a more representative coalition by which to influence this Nation's political activities. The establishment of this coalition is in response to our belief that hyper-partisan extremists have usurped control of our political system and that it has become non-responsive to the needs or desires of the majority of it population.

It is only by organizing our efforts in the form of a political action group that we feel it is possible to re-energize and increase the participation of those citizens who have become dis-enfranchised under the current state of our union. It is our further intention to provide opportunities for all citizens to become more actively engaged participants in their own Self Government. By establishing this group and working together to achieve these goals, our hope is to restore control of this government back into the hands of the people where it belongs and was originally intended.

It is with this basic agreement that we define our core beliefs as follows:

~ We do not require nor adhere to any preexisting political ideology.

~ We are diverse - ethnically, geographically, socially, politically, in age and in experience. We see diversity as strength, not a weakness.

~ We are committed to the principle of inclusion regardless of past or current affiliation.

~ We are 100% grassroots. No lobbyists allowed. No pundits permitted.

~ We encourage reasonable deliberation amongst as many viewpoints as may be available or offered, by members of this or ANY other political party, in order to achieve maximum common good.

~ We believe that politics is the art of compromise. That no single party has all the answers. And that the true measure of political success is when solutions result from maximum participation and minimum alienation of citizens working together towards achieving maximum common good.

~ We believe that honest consideration and debate from multiple points of view is potentially the only true means of achieving bi-partisan solutions to our issues as a nation. We further believe that bi-partisanship is the logical method to ensure maximum common good is achieved.

~ We demand a government that responds to the needs of the majority of its citizens as expressed in the manner defined by the Declaration of Independence, Constitution of the United States and Bill of Rights. NOT corporate interests as expressed by misleading advertising and excessive campaign contributions.

~ We believe our country's best interests are served when the government is made up of people acting independently of mainstream political parties, corporations, and political lobbying networks.

~ We believe all efforts and activities by members of this organization should be carried out in the spirit of voluntarism and social responsibility.

~ We are committed to the transformation of our current political system into a force that will return our nation to the Centrist course of popular governance best stated as; "of the People, by the People, for the People."

~ We want a society in which the concept of democracy is treated as sacrosanct and ordinary citizens participate out of a sense of civic duty, civic pride, and a desire to contribute to society.

~ We are a spontaneous and collective expression of our desire to forge a culture of civic engagement that is first and foremost solution-oriented.

~ We are committed to the concept of allowing the Federal Government to exist as the means in which the individual states within this Nation centralize their activities on behalf of their citizens such as providing a military force, defending national borders and our interests abroad, and to ensure the general safety of its population. Its size should not exceed what is granted to it by the states in order to effectively administer its mandate.

~ We believe in personal, professional and political accountability. We hold ourselves, our peers, predecessors, and allies to the highest possible ethical standards in all actions taken on behalf of this group, in the pursuit of our goals, and in the performance of duties by or on behalf of this nation.

Our Founders gave us an enduring gift - Democracy - We must use it to meet the challenges that we face as a nation as we enter the 21st Century and beyond.

~~~####~~~

We define ourselves as "centrists" because we understand that the "center" is the true power base of politics, especially in a system that has limited itself to only two parties. We have both liberal and conservative leanings and believe strongly in the fact that all voices must be heard before the proper course of action can be decided upon. We espouse a "middle ground" regarding government control and personal behavior. Depending on the issue, we sometimes favor government intervention and sometimes support individual freedom of choice. As Centrists, we pride ourselves on keeping an open mind, we tend to oppose "political extremes," and emphasize what we describe as "practical" solutions to problems. And finally, we believe in the concept of; "Not Left. Not Right. Forward!" as what is needed to fix our system today. By choosing to define ourselves as "non-aligned" with any existing political party, we believe we stand the best chance of creating an environment that fosters change. Here are a few of our public positions:

LEAGUE OF NON-ALIGNED VOTERS
~ <u>POSITION STATEMENTS</u> ~

<u>Abortion </u>- the Party believes in choice. We believe that ultimately this is a decision between a woman and a man, not the government. Although we would prefer other options be explored first, we respect the right of citizen's self-determination.

Border Security - the Party believes that a conservative approach to our national borders is necessary for public safety and legitimizes the immigration process.

Child Labor - the Party adamantly opposes child labor, except in particular family circumstances such as farming and shop keeping.

Corporate Tax - the Party supports reasonable and progressive levels of taxation on corporations as long as innovation and technology are not stifled.

Crime - the Party believes that a strong criminal justice system, which defines the penalty, apprehends alleged criminals and incarcerates those found guilty, is the only real way of deterring crime. Three strike laws, mandatory minimums and other emotionally driven legislation tend to be racist in their application and do not fall in line with the intent of the 14th amendment, and as such should be re-assessed.

Civil Rights - the party believes strongly that all people are created equal, but through circumstances beyond an individual's ability to control, not everyone is treated equal by society. In an attempt to correct this in-equity of treatment, the party supports creative options, including quotas and affirmative action type programs as temporary and periodically reviewed measures until social perspectives adjust. Furthermore, the government must ensure every citizen has access to proper recourse when civil rights violations occur.

Death Penalty - the Party opposes all forms of capital punishment. It should be rarely ever acceptable to take a life. An "eye for an eye" society does nothing but leave everyone blind.

Defense - the Party believes in a strong volunteer military. Used solely to defend the nations interests and, in accordance with international policy or under treaty agreements, those of our allies. Defense funding should remain one of the top priorities to ensure basic safety to the citizens of this country. Decisions regarding using our military as a global police force or otherwise placing them in harm's way should not be made lightly.

Education - the Party believes that all lawful citizens have the right to a world-class education. The Party is committed to ensuring that children have access to the best possible schools, either public or private, and a qualified teaching staff regardless of economic or geographic considerations. It is also imperative that adults have access to continuing education options in order to improve their professional situation.

Environment - the Party believes that the earth is the only home we have and should be treated with respect. This country is 5% of the world population yet leads the world in conspicuous consumption (25%) of raw materials and natural resources. Americans have developed a 'disposable' mentality regarding the environment. We believe this needs to change.

Energy and Oil - the Party strongly supports reducing our consumption of fossil fuels and our dependence on the unstable regions and governments that control these resources. We strongly support research and development of renewable technologies and alternate transportation systems whether in this country or around the globe.

Estate Tax - the Party supports a reasonable estate tax. We propose that "Estates" are not individuals. But individuals can be estates. Therefore, we feel that any taxes generated from "non-individual" sources would seem to be a preferable solution for covering the governments' general spending shortfalls.

Euthanasia - the Party supports the right to die in individual cases. Our preference is always that it would be used only as a last option, but we respect the right of a citizen's self-determination.

Entitlement Programs - the party believes that these programs are in fact a drain on our society, but that they serve a very necessary purpose. Ultimately, we believe that they are fundamentally American. As such, these programs should be safe guarded and the funding generated by a specific tax must remain in the appropriate trust account and not used to cover general spending shortfalls. Any proposed legislation attempting to modify these programs should be put to public vote, not a congressional vote.

Election Reform - the Party is convinced that serious reform is needed to restore and ensure the future integrity of the democratic process. Accountability, spending caps, financial disclosure, shorter campaign cycles, complete process transparency and higher levels of personal integrity are only a few areas that need to be addressed. Fundamental change needs to occur in our election process.

Foreign Investments - the Party endorses and encourages the right of foreign companies to invest in our country under regulation.

Free Trade - the Party supports free trade around the world as an engine to increase the standards of living in the poorest countries. Normalization and regulations must be in place, with the legal authority required, to ensure fairness and standards are applied equally. Exploitation of cheap labor or gaining advantage from a lack of environmental regulations should not be considered acceptable under these agreements

Foreign Policy - the Party understands our place in the world as the last so-called "superpower". This nation has a unique opportunity to lead by example while promoting and assisting developing democratic countries around the world as they attempt self-determination. Therefore, the Party believes that the application of our policies needs to be more democratically implemented so as not to arouse negative opinion or create possible enemies around the world.

Gambling - the Party supports the right to gamble, but also favors high levels of regulation on the gaming industry.

Government Reform - the Party is in favor of updating the electoral, legislative, judicial and executive processes to reflect the realities of the 21st century. This government was originally structured around a country that did not have electric lights, telephones, cars, trains, airplanes or the Internet. It is in this country's best interest to use the available technology to achieve this reform. Cautious awareness must be used to ensure the continued integrity of the process.

Global Warming - the Party is in favor of doing whatever necessary to stabilize the environmental issues facing this planet today. Curbing the amount of greenhouse gases and stopping the progress of global warming are only the tip of the iceberg that must be addressed. International treaties and restrictions such as Kyoto are good first steps in this process.

Gun Control - the Party supports gun control to the extent that people still have the right to own guns although under minimal restriction. Common sense and practical necessity regarding public safety should lead the way.

Immigration - the Party supports a centrist approach to allowing immigrants the right to seek naturalization in the manner determined to be appropriate by congress. We are a country founded by people from other countries who sought a fresh start. We respect and admire those who follow that tradition.

Labor Unions - the Party supports the right of labor unions to exist as a means to provide a voice for the workers to secure decent wages, benefits and collective bargaining power.

Media Consolidation - the Party encourages the growth of more autonomous and independent media outlets. Likewise, the party believes in the regulation of media ownership to avoid monopolies on public information. There are at least three sides to every tale; Side A, Side B and Reality. In this respect, more is indeed better.

Nuclear Armament - the Party recognizes nuclear arms and energy are here to stay and cannot be un-invented. As such, the party believes in strong regulation of the industry and encourages vigorous research into safer equipment, facilities and cleaner forms of power generation.

Pornography - the Party supports the right of the porn industry to exist, though under severe regulations.

Privatization - the Party believes there needs to be an active and competitive private sector; sufficiently regulated so long as innovation and technology are not stifled.

Right to Privacy - the Party believes deeply in the individual's right to privacy and that this right shall be extended, protected and defended, for all persons lawfully residing in this country. Collection and sale of private information should be restricted.

Same-Sex Marriage - the Party believes that all people -- all races, all religions, and all sexual orientations -- have the right to legal Marriage to the person of their choice. All people are also entitled to all the rights and benefits that follow. No other classification shall be allowed as a substitute. "Separate but equal" legislation has been tried before and not only failed, but was ruled unconstitutional.

Social Security - the Party believes social programs like this show what is good and right in America today. However, through the mismanagement of elected officials, this program has real problems that must be addressed soon. Social Security tax funds received into the trust fund must be considered un-touchable and used only by the program to pay out benefit claims, not for use to cover general spending shortfalls. This government made a commitment to its citizens and it must correct the problems it created in order to live up to this great promise.

Separation of Church and State - the Party believes in a clear divide between these two entities, but also recognizes the fact that the two will cross paths periodically. Dispositions regarding items like public monuments, sworn oaths and other potential crossover areas should be left up to the communities in which they occur.

Stem Cell Research - the Party is sensitive to the fact that science and religion have historically come into conflict with each other for various reasons. Therefore, it is our position that science, being sensitive to the moral objections of non-scientists, should be allowed to pursue beneficial knowledge by using cells obtained from legally and ethically approved sources under strict regulation. The Party does reserve the right to amend this position as new information becomes available.

Tax Reform - the Party strongly supports the abolition of the current form of individual income tax. Although, the party supports the concept of a tax on individual income ONLY as long as it adheres the rules laid out in the founding documents

Universal Suffrage - the Party supports the right of all men and women, after achieving a certain age, the right to vote.

War on Drugs - the Party believes that the illegalization of both soft and hard drugs should remain in effect, but that there needs to be a fundamental shift in the hearts and minds of legislators and the law enforcement community from that of crime/ punishment to education/recovery programs.

War on Poverty - the Party believes that anyone holding a full time job, with benefits, should be earning enough pay to not be living in poverty. The existence of basic Social safety nets is supported under strict oversight. These programs, in conjunction with private charitable groups, should work ensure no citizen goes without basic human material needs.

As I close this book, I have only one question to ask; Are you tired of politics as usual? If you willing to do something to try to fix the problems facing this nation today, and if you willing to leave your comfort zone to make it happen, then we would like to hear from you. Please take a moment and send your comments regarding this book, or any ideas you have to effect change in our government, to me personally. Send all comments and requests to *me@ejkiser.com* or check me out on FaceBook.

Thank you for your time and God Bless the United States of America.

EJK

Connect with me online:
www.forgottencostoffreedom.com
Smashwords Author page
www.ejkiser.com
or
FaceBook

APPENDICES

Appendix 1

THE DECLARATION OF INDEPENDENCE

IN CONGRESS, JULY 4, 1776

The unanimous Declaration of the thirteen united States of America

When in the Course of human events it becomes necessary for one people to dissolve the political bands which have connected them with another and to assume among the powers of the earth, the separate and equal station to which the Laws of Nature and of Nature's God entitle them, a decent respect to the opinions of mankind requires that they should declare the causes which impel them to the separation.

We hold these truths to be self-evident, that all men are created equal, that they are endowed by their Creator with certain unalienable Rights, that among these are Life, Liberty and the pursuit of Happiness. — That to secure these rights, Governments are instituted among Men, deriving their just powers from the consent of the governed, — That whenever any Form of Government becomes destructive of these ends, it is the Right of the People to alter or to abolish it, and to institute new Government, laying its foundation on such principles and organizing its powers in such form, as to them shall seem most likely to affect their Safety and Happiness. Prudence, indeed, will dictate that Governments long established should not be changed for light and transient causes; and accordingly all experience hath shewn that mankind are more disposed to suffer, while evils are sufferable than to right themselves by abolishing the forms to which they are accustomed. But when a long train of abuses and usurpations, pursuing invariably the same Object evinces a design to reduce them under absolute Despotism, it is their right, it is their duty, to throw off such Government, and to provide new Guards for their future security. — Such has been the patient sufferance of these Colonies; and such is now the necessity which constrains them to alter their former Systems of Government. The history of the present King of Great Britain is a history of repeated injuries and usurpations, all having in direct object the establishment of an absolute Tyranny over these States. To prove this, let Facts be submitted to a candid world.

~ He has refused his Assent to Laws, the most wholesome and necessary for the public good.

~ He has forbidden his Governors to pass Laws of immediate and pressing importance, unless suspended in their operation till his Assent should be obtained; and when so suspended, he has utterly neglected to attend to them.

~ He has refused to pass other Laws for the accommodation of large districts of people, unless those people would relinquish the right of Representation in the Legislature, a right inestimable to them and formidable to tyrants only.

~ He has called together legislative bodies at places unusual, uncomfortable, and distant from the depository of their Public Records, for the sole purpose of fatiguing them into compliance with his measures.

~ He has dissolved Representative Houses repeatedly, for opposing with manly firmness his invasions on the rights of the people.

~ He has refused for a long time, after such dissolutions, to cause others to be elected, whereby the Legislative Powers, incapable of Annihilation, have returned to the People at large for their exercise; the State remaining in the mean time exposed to all the dangers of invasion from without, and convulsions within.

~ He has endeavoured to prevent the population of these States; for that purpose obstructing the Laws for Naturalization of Foreigners; refusing to pass others to encourage their migrations hither, and raising the conditions of new Appropriations of Lands.

~ He has obstructed the Administration of Justice by refusing his Assent to Laws for establishing Judiciary Powers.

~ He has made Judges dependent on his Will alone for the tenure of their offices, and the amount and payment of their salaries.

~ He has erected a multitude of New Offices, and sent hither swarms of Officers to harass our people and eat out their substance.

~ He has kept among us, in times of peace, Standing Armies without the Consent of our legislatures.

~ He has affected to render the Military independent of and superior to the Civil Power.

~ He has combined with others to subject us to a jurisdiction foreign to our constitution, and unacknowledged by our laws; giving his Assent to their Acts of pretended Legislation:

~ For quartering large bodies of armed troops among us:

~ For protecting them, by a mock Trial from punishment for any Murders which they should commit on the Inhabitants of these States:

~ For cutting off our Trade with all parts of the world:

~ For imposing Taxes on us without our Consent:

~ For depriving us in many cases, of the benefit of Trial by Jury:

~ For transporting us beyond Seas to be tried for pretended offences:

~ For abolishing the free System of English Laws in a neighboring Province, establishing therein an Arbitrary government, and enlarging its Boundaries so as to render it at once an example and fit instrument for introducing the same absolute rule onto these Colonies

~ For taking away our Charters, abolishing our most valuable Laws and altering fundamentally the Forms of our Governments:

~ For suspending our own Legislatures, and declaring themselves invested with power to legislate for us in all cases whatsoever.

~ He has abdicated Government here, by declaring us out of his Protection and waging War against us.

~ He has plundered our seas, ravaged our coasts, burnt our towns, and destroyed the lives of our people.

~ He is at this time transporting large Armies of foreign Mercenaries to compleat the works of death, desolation, and tyranny, already begun with circumstances of Cruelty & Perfidy scarcely paralleled in the most barbarous ages, and totally unworthy the Head of a civilized nation.

~ He has constrained our fellow Citizens taken Captive on the high Seas to bear Arms against their Country, to become the executioners of their friends and Brethren, or to fall themselves by their Hands.

~ He has excited domestic insurrections amongst us, and has endeavoured to bring on the inhabitants of our frontiers, the merciless Indian Savages whose known rule of warfare, is an undistinguished destruction of all ages, sexes and conditions.

In every stage of these Oppressions We have Petitioned for Redress in the most humble terms: Our repeated Petitions have been answered only by repeated injury. A Prince, whose character is thus marked by every act which may define a Tyrant, is unfit to be the ruler of a free people.

Nor have We been wanting in attentions to our British brethren. We have warned them from time to time of attempts by their legislature to extend an unwarrantable jurisdiction over us. We have reminded them of the circumstances of our emigration and settlement here. We have appealed to their native justice and magnanimity, and we have conjured them by the ties of our common kindred to disavow these usurpations, which would inevitably interrupt our connections and correspondence. They too have been deaf to the voice of justice and of consanguinity. We must, therefore, acquiesce in the necessity, which denounces our Separation, and hold them, as we hold the rest of mankind, Enemies in War, in Peace Friends.

We, therefore, the Representatives of the united States of America, in General Congress, Assembled, appealing to the Supreme Judge of the world for the rectitude of our intentions, do, in the Name, and by Authority of the good People of these Colonies, solemnly publish and declare, That these united Colonies are, and of Right ought to be Free and Independent States, that they are Absolved from all Allegiance to the British Crown, and that all political connection between them and the State of Great Britain, is and ought to be totally dissolved; and that as Free and Independent States, they have null Power to levy War, conclude Peace, contract Alliances, establish Commerce, and to do all other Acts and Things which Independent States may of right do. — And for the support of this Declaration, with a firm reliance on the protection of Divine Providence, we mutually pledge to each other our Lives, our Fortunes, and our sacred Honor.

Appendix 2

THE CONSTITUTION OF THE UNITED STATES

WE THE PEOPLE of the United States, in Order to form a more perfect Union, establish Justice, insure domestic Tranquility, provide for the common defence, promote the general Welfare, and secure the Blessings of Liberty to ourselves and our Posterity, do ordain and establish this Constitution for the United States of America.

Article. I.

Section. I.

All legislative Powers herein granted shall be vested in a Congress of the United States, which shall consist of a Senate and House of Representatives.

Section. II.

The House of Representatives shall be composed of Members chosen every second Year by the People of the several States, and the Electors in each State shall have the Qualifications requisite for Electors of the most numerous Branch of the State Legislature.

No Person shall be a Representative who shall not have attained to the Age of twenty five Years, and been seven Years a Citizen of the United States, and who shall not, when elected, be an Inhabitant of that State in which he shall be chosen.

Representatives and direct Taxes shall be apportioned among the several States which may be included within this Union, according to their respective Numbers, which shall be determined by adding to the whole Number of free Persons, including those bound to Service for a Term of Years, and excluding Indians not taxed, three fifths of all other Persons.

The actual Enumeration shall be made within three Years after the first Meeting of the Congress of the United States, and within every subsequent Term of ten Years, in such Manner as they shall by Law direct. The Number of Representatives shall not exceed one for every thirty Thousand, but each State shall have at Least one Representative; and until such enumeration shall be made, the State of New Hampshire shall be entitled to chuse three, Massachusetts eight, Rhode-Island and Providence Plantations one, Connecticut five, New-York six, New Jersey four, Pennsylvania eight, Delaware one, Maryland six, Virginia ten, North Carolina five, South Carolina five, and Georgia three. When vacancies happen in the Representation from any State, the Executive Authority thereof shall issue Writs of Election to fill such Vacancies.

The House of Representatives shall chuse their Speaker and other Officers; and shall have the sole Power of Impeachment.

Section. III.

The Senate of the United States shall be composed of two Senators from each State, chosen by the Legislature thereof for six Years; and each Senator shall have one Vote.

Immediately after they shall be assembled in Consequence of the first Election, they shall be divided as equally as may be into three Classes.

The Seats of the Senators of the first Class shall be vacated at the Expiration of the second Year, of the second Class at the Expiration of the fourth Year, and of the third Class at the Expiration of the sixth Year, so that one third may be chosen every second Year; and if Vacancies happen by Resignation, or otherwise, during the Recess of the Legislature of any State, the Executive thereof may make temporary Appointments until the next Meeting of the Legislature, which shall then fill such Vacancies.

No Person shall be a Senator who shall not have attained to the Age of thirty Years, and been nine Years a Citizen of the United States, and who shall not, when elected, be an Inhabitant of that State for which he shall be chosen.

The Vice President of the United States shall be President of the Senate, but shall have no Vote, unless they be equally divided.

The Senate shall chuse their other Officers, and also a President pro tempore, in the Absence of the Vice President, or when he shall exercise the Office of President of the United States.

The Senate shall have the sole Power to try all Impeachments. When sitting for that Purpose, they shall be on Oath or Affirmation. When the President of the United States is tried, the Chief Justice shall preside: And no Person shall be convicted without the Concurrence of two thirds of the Members present.

Judgment in Cases of Impeachment shall not extend further than to removal from Office, and disqualification to hold and enjoy any Office of honor, Trust or Profit under the United States: but the Party convicted shall nevertheless be liable and subject to Indictment, Trial, Judgment and Punishment, according to Law.

Section. IV.

The Times, Places and Manner of holding Elections for Senators and Representatives, shall be prescribed in each State by the Legislature thereof; but the Congress may at any time by Law make or alter such Regulations, except as to the Places of chusing Senators.

The Congress shall assemble at least once in every Year, and such Meeting shall be on the first Monday in December, unless they shall by Law appoint a different Day.

Section. V.

Each House shall be the Judge of the Elections, Returns and Qualifications of its own Members, and a Majority of each shall constitute a Quorum to do Business; but a smaller Number may adjourn from day to day, and may be authorized to compel the Attendance of absent Members, in such Manner, and under such Penalties as each House may provide.

Each House may determine the Rules of its Proceedings, punish its Members for disorderly Behaviour, and, with the Concurrence of two thirds, expel a Member.

Each House shall keep a Journal of its Proceedings, and from time to time publish the same, excepting such Parts as may in their Judgment require Secrecy; and the Yeas and Nays of the Members of either House on any question shall, at the Desire of one fifth of those Present, be entered on the Journal.

Neither House, during the Session of Congress, shall, without the Consent of the other, adjourn for more than three days, nor to any other Place than that in which the two Houses shall be sitting.

Section. VI.

The Senators and Representatives shall receive a Compensation for their Services, to be ascertained by Law, and paid out of the Treasury of the United States. They shall in all Cases, except Treason, Felony and Breach of the Peace, be privileged from Arrest during their Attendance at the Session of their respective Houses, and in going to and returning from the same; and for any Speech or Debate in either House, they shall not be questioned in any other Place.

No Senator or Representative shall, during the Time for which he was elected, be appointed to any civil Office under the Authority of the United States, which shall have been created, or the Emoluments whereof shall have been increased during such time; and no Person holding any Office under the United States, shall be a Member of either House during his Continuance in Office.

Section. VII.

All Bills for raising Revenue shall originate in the House of Representatives; but the Senate may propose or concur with Amendments as on other Bills.

Every Bill which shall have passed the House of Representatives and the Senate, shall, before it become a Law, be presented to the President of the United States: If he approve he shall sign it, but if not he shall return it, with his Objections to that House in which it shall have originated, who shall enter the Objections at large on their Journal, and proceed to reconsider it. If after such Reconsideration two thirds of that House shall agree to pass the Bill, it shall be sent, together with the Objections, to the other House, by which it shall likewise be reconsidered, and if approved by two thirds of that House, it shall become a Law. But in all such Cases the Votes of both Houses shall be determined by yeas and Nays, and the Names of the Persons voting for and against the Bill shall be entered on the Journal of each House respectively. If any Bill shall not be returned by the President within ten Days (Sundays excepted) after it shall have been presented to him, the Same shall be a Law, in like Manner as if he had signed it, unless the

Congress by their Adjournment prevent its Return, in which Case it shall not be a Law.

Every Order, Resolution, or Vote to which the Concurrence of the Senate and House of Representatives may be necessary (except on a question of Adjournment) shall be presented to the President of the United States; and before the Same shall take Effect, shall be approved by him, or being disapproved by him, shall be repassed by two thirds of the Senate and House of Representatives, according to the Rules and Limitations prescribed in the Case of a Bill.

Section. VIII.

The Congress shall have Power To lay and collect Taxes, Duties, Imposts and Excises, to pay the Debts and provide for the common Defence and general Welfare of the United States; but all Duties, Imposts and Excises shall be uniform throughout the United States;

To borrow Money on the credit of the United States;

To regulate Commerce with foreign Nations, and among the several States, and with the Indian Tribes;

To establish an uniform Rule of Naturalization, and uniform Laws on the subject of Bankruptcies throughout the United States;

To coin Money, regulate the Value thereof, and of foreign Coin, and fix the Standard of Weights and Measures;

To provide for the Punishment of counterfeiting the Securities and current Coin of the United States;

To establish Post Offices and post Roads;

To promote the Progress of Science and useful Arts, by securing for limited Times to Authors and Inventors the exclusive Right to their respective Writings and Discoveries;

To constitute Tribunals inferior to the supreme Court;

To define and punish Piracies and Felonies committed on the high Seas, and Offences against the Law of Nations;

To declare War, grant Letters of Marque and Reprisal, and make Rules concerning Captures on Land and Water;

To raise and support Armies, but no Appropriation of Money to that Use shall be for a longer Term than two Years;

To provide and maintain a Navy;

To make Rules for the Government and Regulation of the land and naval Forces;

To provide for calling forth the Militia to execute the Laws of the Union, suppress Insurrections and repel Invasions;

To provide for organizing, arming, and disciplining, the Militia, and for governing such Part of them as may be employed in the Service of the United States, reserving to the States respectively, the Appointment of the Officers, and the Authority of training the Militia according to the discipline prescribed by Congress;

To exercise exclusive Legislation in all Cases whatsoever, over such District (not exceeding ten Miles square) as may, by Cession of particular States, and the Acceptance of Congress, become the Seat of the Government of the United States, and to exercise like Authority over all Places purchased by the Consent of the Legislature of the State in which the Same shall be, for the Erection of Forts, Magazines, Arsenals, dock-Yards, and other needful Buildings;--And

To make all Laws which shall be necessary and proper for carrying into Execution the foregoing Powers, and all other Powers vested by this Constitution in the Government of the United States, or in any Department or Officer thereof.

Section. IX.

The Migration or Importation of such Persons as any of the States now existing shall think proper to admit, shall not be prohibited by the congress prior to the Year one thousand eight hundred and eight, but a Tax or duty may be imposed on such Importation, not exceeding ten Dollars for each Person.

The Privilege of the Writ of Habeas Corpus shall not be suspended, unless when in Cases of Rebellion or Invasion the public Safety may require it.

No Bill of Attainder or ex post facto Law shall be passed.

No Capitation, or other direct, Tax shall be laid, unless in Proportion to the Census or enumeration herein before directed to be taken.

No Tax or Duty shall be laid on Articles exported from any State.

No Preference shall be given by any Regulation of Commerce or Revenue to the Ports of one State over those of another; nor shall Vessels bound to, or from, one State, be obliged to enter, clear, or pay Duties in another.

No Money shall be drawn from the Treasury, but in Consequence of Appropriations made by Law; and a regular Statement and Account of the Receipts and Expenditures of all public Money shall be published from time to time.

No Title of Nobility shall be granted by the United States: And no Person holding any Office of Profit or Trust under them, shall, without the Consent of the Congress, accept of any present, Emolument, Office, or Title, of any kind whatever, from any King, Prince, or foreign State.

Section. X.

No State shall enter into any Treaty, Alliance, or Confederation; grant Letters of Marque and Reprisal; coin Money; emit Bills of Credit; make any Thing but gold and silver Coin a Tender in Payment of Debts; pass any Bill of Attainder, ex post facto Law, or Law impairing the Obligation of Contracts, or grant any Title of Nobility.

No State shall, without the Consent of the Congress, lay any Imposts or Duties on Imports or Exports, except what may be absolutely necessary for executing it's inspection Laws: and the net Produce of all Duties and Imposts, laid by any State on Imports or Exports, shall be for the Use of the Treasury of the United States; and all such Laws shall be subject to the Revision and Controul of the Congress.

No State shall, without the Consent of Congress, lay any Duty of Tonnage, keep Troops, or Ships of War in time of Peace, enter into any Agreement or Compact with another State, or with a foreign Power, or engage in War, unless actually invaded, or in such imminent Danger as will not admit of delay.

Article. II.

Section. I.

The executive Power shall be vested in a President of the United States of America. He shall hold his Office during the Term of four Years, and, together with the Vice President, chosen for the same Term, be elected, as follows:

Each State shall appoint, in such Manner as the Legislature thereof may direct, a Number of Electors, equal to the whole Number of Senators and Representatives to which the State may be entitled in the Congress: but no Senator or Representative, or Person holding an Office of Trust or Profit under the United States, shall be appointed an Elector.

The Electors shall meet in their respective States, and vote by Ballot for two Persons, of whom one at least shall not be an Inhabitant of the same State with themselves. And they shall make a List of all the Persons voted for, and of the Number of Votes for each; which List they shall sign and certify, and transmit sealed to the Seat of the Government of the United States, directed to the President of the Senate. The President of the Senate shall, in the Presence of the Senate and House of

Representatives, open all the Certificates, and the Votes shall then be counted. The Person having the greatest Number of Votes shall be the President, if such Number be a Majority of the whole Number of Electors appointed; and if there be more than one who have such Majority, and have an equal Number of Votes, then the House of Representatives shall immediately chuse by Ballot one of them for President; and if no Person have a Majority, then from the five highest on the List the said House shall in like Manner chuse the President. But in chusing the President, the Votes shall be taken by States, the Representation from each State having one Vote; A quorum for this purpose shall consist of a Member or Members from two thirds of the States, and a Majority of all the States shall be necessary to a Choice. In every Case, after the Choice of the President, the Person having the greatest Number of Votes of the Electors shall be the Vice President. But if there should remain two or more who have equal Votes, the Senate shall chuse from them by Ballot the Vice President.

The Congress may determine the Time of chusing the Electors, and the Day on which they shall give their Votes; which Day shall be the same throughout the United States.

No Person except a natural born Citizen, or a Citizen of the United States, at the time of the Adoption of this Constitution, shall be eligible to the Office of President; neither shall any Person be eligible to that Office who shall not have attained to the Age of thirty five Years, and been fourteen Years a Resident within the United States.

In Case of the Removal of the President from Office, or of his Death, Resignation, or Inability to discharge the Powers and Duties of the said Office, the Same shall devolve on the Vice President, and the Congress may by Law provide for the Case of Removal, Death, Resignation or Inability, both of the President and Vice President, declaring what Officer shall then act as President, and such Officer shall act accordingly, until the Disability be removed, or a President shall be elected.

The President shall, at stated Times, receive for his Services, a Compensation, which shall neither be increased nor diminished during the Period for which he shall have been elected, and he shall not receive within that Period any other Emolument from the United States, or any of them.

Before he enter on the Execution of his Office, he shall take the following Oath or Affirmation:--"I do solemnly swear (or affirm) that I will faithfully execute the Office of President of the United States, and will to the best of my Ability, preserve, protect and defend the Constitution of the United States."

Section. II.

The President shall be Commander in Chief of the Army and Navy of the United States, and of the Militia of the several States, when called into the actual Service of the United States; he may require the Opinion, in writing, of the principal Officer in each of the executive Departments, upon any Subject relating to the Duties of their respective Offices, and he shall have Power to grant Reprieves and Pardons for Offences against the United States, except in Cases of Impeachment.

He shall have Power, by and with the Advice and Consent of the Senate, to make Treaties, provided two thirds of the Senators present concur; and he shall nominate, and by and with the Advice and Consent of the Senate, shall appoint Ambassadors, other public Ministers and Consuls, Judges of the supreme Court, and all other Officers of the United States, whose Appointments are not herein otherwise provided for, and which shall be established by Law: but the Congress may by Law vest the Appointment of such inferior Officers, as they think proper, in the President alone, in the Courts of Law, or in the Heads of Departments.

The President shall have Power to fill up all Vacancies that may happen during the Recess of the Senate, by granting Commissions which shall expire at the End of their next Session.

Section. III.

He shall from time to time give to the Congress Information of the State of the Union, and recommend to their Consideration such Measures as he shall judge necessary and expedient; he may, on extraordinary Occasions, convene both Houses, or either of them, and in Case of Disagreement between them, with Respect to the Time of Adjournment, he may adjourn them to such Time as he shall think proper; he shall receive Ambassadors and other public Ministers; he shall take Care that the Laws be faithfully executed, and shall Commission all the Officers of the United States.

Section. IV.

The President, Vice President and all civil Officers of the United States, shall be removed from Office on Impeachment for, and Conviction of, Treason, Bribery, or other high Crimes and Misdemeanors.

Article III.

Section. I.

The judicial Power of the United States shall be vested in one supreme Court, and in such inferior Courts as the Congress may from time to time ordain and establish. The Judges, both of the supreme and inferior Courts, shall hold their Offices during good Behaviour, and shall, at stated Times, receive for their Services a Compensation, which shall not be diminished during their Continuance in Office.

Section. II.

The judicial Power shall extend to all Cases, in Law and Equity, arising under this Constitution, the Laws of the United States, and Treaties made, or which shall be made, under their Authority;--to all Cases affecting Ambassadors, other public Ministers and Consuls;--to all Cases of admiralty and maritime Jurisdiction;--to Controversies to which the United States shall be a Party;--to Controversies between two or more States;-- between a State and Citizens of another State,--between Citizens of different States,--between Citizens of the same State claiming Lands under Grants of different States, and between a State, or the Citizens thereof, and foreign States, Citizens or Subjects.

In all Cases affecting Ambassadors, other public Ministers and Consuls, and those in which a State shall be Party, the supreme Court shall have original Jurisdiction. In all the other Cases before mentioned, the supreme Court shall have appellate Jurisdiction, both as to Law and Fact, with such Exceptions, and under such Regulations as the Congress shall make.

The Trial of all Crimes, except in Cases of Impeachment, shall be by Jury; and such Trial shall be held in the State where the said Crimes shall have been committed; but when not committed within any State, the Trial shall be at such Place or Places as the Congress may by Law have directed.

Section. III.

Treason against the United States, shall consist only in levying Warn against them, or in adhering to their Enemies, giving them Aid and Comfort. No Person shall be convicted of Treason unless on the Testimony of two Witnesses to the same overt Act, or on Confession in open Court.

The Congress shall have Power to declare the Punishment of Treason, but no Attainder of Treason shall work Corruption of Blood, or Forfeiture except during the Life of the Person attainted.

Article. IV.

Section. I.

Full Faith and Credit shall be given in each State to the public Acts, Records, and judicial Proceedings of every other State. And the

Congress may by general Laws prescribe the Manner in which such Acts, Records and Proceedings shall be proved, and the Effect thereof.

Section. II.

The Citizens of each State shall be entitled to all Privileges and Immunities of Citizens in the several States. A Person charged in any State with Treason, Felony, or other Crime, who shall flee from Justice, and be found in another State, shall on Demand of the executive Authority of the State from which he fled, be delivered up, to be removed to the State having Jurisdiction of the Crime.

No Person held to Service or Labour in one State, under the Laws thereof, escaping into another, shall, in Consequence of any Law or Regulation therein, be discharged from such Service or Labour, but shall be delivered up on Claim of the Party to whom such Service or Labour may be due.

Section. III.

New States may be admitted by the Congress into this Union; but no new State shall be formed or erected within the Jurisdiction of any other State; nor any State be formed by the Junction of two or more States, or Parts of States, without the Consent of the Legislatures of the States concerned as well as of the Congress.

The Congress shall have Power to dispose of and make all needful Rules and Regulations respecting the Territory or other Property belonging to the United States; and nothing in this Constitution shall be so construed as to Prejudice any Claims of the United States, or of any particular State.

Section. IV.

The United States shall guarantee to every State in this Union a Republican Form of Government, and shall protect each of them against Invasion; and on Application of the Legislature, or of the Executive (when the Legislature cannot be convened), against domestic Violence.

Article. V.

The Congress, whenever two thirds of both Houses shall deem it necessary, shall propose Amendments to this Constitution, or, on the Application of the Legislatures of two thirds of the several States, shall call a Convention for proposing Amendments, which, in either Case, shall be valid to all Intents and Purposes, as Part of this Constitution, when ratified by the Legislatures of three fourths of the several States, or by Conventions in three fourths thereof, as the one or the other Mode of Ratification may be proposed by the Congress; Provided that no Amendment which may be made prior to the Year One thousand eight hundred and eight shall in any Manner affect the first and fourth Clauses in the Ninth Section of the first Article; and that no State, without its Consent, shall be deprived of its equal Suffrage in the Senate.

Article. VI.

All Debts contracted and Engagements entered into, before the Adoption of this Constitution, shall be as valid against the United States under this Constitution, as under the Confederation.

This Constitution, and the Laws of the United States which shall be made in Pursuance thereof; and all Treaties made, or which shall be made, under the Authority of the United States, shall be the supreme Law of the Land; and the Judges in every State shall be bound thereby, any Thing in the Constitution or Laws of any State to the Contrary notwithstanding.

The Senators and Representatives before mentioned, and the Members of the several State Legislatures, and all executive and judicial Officers, both of the United States and of the several States, shall be bound by Oath or Affirmation, to support this Constitution; but no religious Test shall ever be required as a Qualification to any Office or public Trust under the United States.

Article. VII.

The Ratification of the Conventions of nine States, shall be sufficient for the Establishment of this Constitution between the States so ratifying the Same.

The Word, "the," being interlined between the seventh and eighth Lines of the first Page, the Word "Thirty" being partly written on an Erazure in the fifteenth Line of the first Page, The Words "is tried" being interlined between the thirty second and thirty third Lines of the first Page and the Word "the" being interlined between the forty third and forty fourth Lines of the second Page.

Attest William Jackson Secretary done in Convention by the Unanimous Consent of the States present the Seventeenth Day of September in the Year of our Lord one thousand seven hundred and Eighty seven and of the Independance of the United States of America the Twelfth In witness whereof We have hereunto subscribed our Names,

.

152

Appendix 3

THE BILL OF RIGHTS

The Preamble to The Bill of Rights

Congress of the United States begun and held at the City of New-York, on Wednesday the fourth of March, one thousand seven hundred and eighty nine.

THE Conventions of a number of the States, having at the time of their adopting the Constitution, expressed a desire, in order to prevent misconstruction or abuse of its powers, that further declaratory and restrictive clauses should be added: And as extending the ground of public confidence in the Government, will best ensure the beneficent ends of its institution.

RESOLVED by the Senate and House of Representatives of the United States of America, in Congress assembled, two thirds of both Houses concurring, that the following Articles be proposed to the Legislatures of the several States, as amendments to the Constitution of the United States, all, or any of which Articles, when ratified by three fourths of the said Legislatures, to be valid to all intents and purposes, as part of the said Constitution; viz.

ARTICLES in addition to, and Amendment of the Constitution of the United States of America, proposed by Congress, and ratified by the Legislatures of the several States, pursuant to the fifth Article of the original Constitution.

Amendment I

Congress shall make no law respecting an establishment of religion, or prohibiting the free exercise thereof; or abridging the freedom of speech, or of the press; or the right of the people peaceably to assemble, and to petition the Government for a redress of grievances.

Amendment II

A well regulated Militia, being necessary to the security of a free State, the right of the people to keep and bear Arms, shall not be infringed.

Amendment III

No Soldier shall, in time of peace be quartered in any house, without the consent of the Owner, nor in time of war, but in a manner to be prescribed by law.

Amendment IV

The right of the people to be secure in their persons, houses, papers, and effects, against unreasonable searches and seizures, shall not be violated, and no Warrants shall issue, but upon probable cause, supported by Oath or affirmation, and particularly describing the place to be searched, and the persons or things to be seized.

Amendment V

No person shall be held to answer for a capital, or otherwise infamous crime, unless on a presentment or indictment of a Grand Jury, except in cases arising in the land or naval forces, or in the Militia, when in actual service in time of War or public danger; nor shall any person be subject for the same offence to be twice put in jeopardy of life or limb; nor shall be compelled in any criminal case to be a witness against himself, nor be deprived of life, liberty, or property, without due process of law; nor shall private property be taken for public use, without just compensation.

Amendment VI

In all criminal prosecutions, the accused shall enjoy the right to a speedy and public trial, by an impartial jury of the State and district wherein the crime shall have been committed, which district shall have been previously ascertained by law, and to be informed of the nature and cause of the accusation; to be confronted with the witnesses against him; to have compulsory process for obtaining witnesses in his favor, and to have the Assistance of Counsel for his defence.

Amendment VII

In Suits at common law, where the value in controversy shall exceed twenty dollars, the right of trial by jury shall be preserved, and no fact tried by a jury, shall be otherwise re-examined in any Court of the United States, than according to the rules of the common law.

Amendment VIII

Excessive bail shall not be required, nor excessive fines imposed, nor cruel and unusual punishments inflicted.

Amendment IX

The enumeration in the Constitution, of certain rights, shall not be construed to deny or disparage others retained by the people.

Amendment X

The powers not delegated to the United States by the Constitution, nor prohibited by

ABOUT THE AUTHOR

Eric J. Kiser

Mr. Kiser is an average American citizen who has become concerned about the political division taking hold in this country over the last quarter century. He is a life-long student of history and human behavior and has spent more than 20 years heading up various projects in the music, film and television industry. His latest project is the documentary film "On Dangerous Ground" which focuses on the problems of peak oil and climate change. He lives in San Diego, CA